W9-AZI-521

*Helping
the Helpers
to Help*

By Ruth B. Caplan

Psychiatry and the Community in Nineteenth Century America

HELPING
THE HELPERS
TO HELP

Mental Health Consultation to
Aid Clergymen in Pastoral Work

by RUTH B. CAPLAN

in collaboration with
Gerald Caplan, David E. Richards,
and Anson Phelps Stokes, Jr.

THE SEABURY PRESS · NEW YORK

The House of Bishops Committee on Pastoral Development gratefully acknowledges the financial assistance received toward the publication of this study from The Academy of Religion and Mental Health.

Library of Congress Catalog Card Number: 72-81024
ISBN: 0-8164-0239-6
755-972-C-5
Design by Carol Basen
Printed in the United States of America

For my mother,
Ann Caplan,
who always helps.

Preface

Despite the secular nature of these times and the growth of helping agencies outside the churches, it is still true that people in trouble often turn first to priests, ministers, and rabbis for guidance and help. There is consequent concern in lay, ecclesiastical, and mental health circles that clergymen have some form of continuing education and support that will enable them to cope with the many complex human situations which they encounter in their daily work.

This book describes a mental health consultation program that was established by the Episcopal Diocese of Massachusetts and the Harvard Medical School Laboratory of Community Psychiatry to try to meet this need. Clergy of all denominations might be interested to learn of the existence of this service, for as our interviews with rabbis, Catholic priests, and ministers of various Protestant churches have shown us, many professional problems are generic, and might therefore be eased by similar methods.

Consultation is unusual among mental services in that it focuses not on the traditional psychiatric role of diagnosing the mentally disturbed of the parish and referring them for treatment, but rather, on supporting the minister in his own management of bewildering cases in which mental health issues beyond his current expertise are blocking his effectiveness. The aim of this program has been to help clergy develop greater skill, confidence, and objectivity in handling such cases, so that they will grow more self-reliant and effective in aiding particular members of their congregation, as well as others, with similar problems, in the future.

As will be seen presently, consultation, unlike other programs intended to increase the sophistication of clergy about emotional issues, studiously avoids dealing explicitly with the personal problems of ministers. Consultation is not psychotherapy. The format, in both individual and group sessions, is restricted to discussing the problems of parishioners and the organizational and social difficulties of the parish. The system is designed never to threaten the privacy of consultees. Nevertheless, successful consultation is not a purely intellectual experience. It can contribute indirectly to the emotional well-being of the minister, and to his personal sense of competence and worth.

This account of the consultation program in Massachusetts is also addressed to psychiatrists, psychologists, social workers, and laymen concerned with mental health. The 1963 Federal Community Mental Health Act directed that such consultation services be provided by all community mental health centers to backstop colleagues in other caregiving professions. Since this form of consultation is new to many in the mental health field, and since some of the work problems of clergy are unique, this book may widen the perspective of clinicians interested in working with ministers. It offers them the experience of the Harvard Medical School consultants both as a guide to productive technique, and as a caution against easy mistakes. It may also minimize the danger, inherent in careless consultation, of unwittingly distorting the pastor's role by forcing on the consultee the techniques and professional values of mental health clinicians, thereby depriving the community of the specialized contributions of its priests.

Since, therefore, the book is intended for so varied an audience, the reader's indulgence is asked if "obvious" points are too laboriously explained, or if mental health terminology is used too often. One of the first problems faced by consultants and consultees is that of learning each other's professional language. Perhaps this book may serve as an introduction to bridge that gap for both parties.

The book will first present a brief history of the origins and development of the collaboration between the Diocese of Massachusetts and the Harvard Laboratory of Community Psychiatry, and an explanation of the theory and techniques of mental health consultation. Next, we will turn to actual examples of the system in action, using disguised case material. The impact of this technique can best be felt in flesh-and-blood situations, for it sounds deceptively tame when its methods are described theoretically. Therefore, anecdotal material is presented here in a highly detailed form. We hope that the greater vividness which this makes possible will compensate for any inadvertent patches of tedium.[1] We conclude this section with an evaluation of the impact of consultation on those who participated in its sessions.

In the next section Dr. Gerald Caplan, Director of the Harvard Laboratory of Community Psychiatry, will describe some outgrowths of the consultation program for parish clergy in his work with the Bishop of Massachusetts and the Episcopal House of Bishops. He will then discuss the implications of the total program for community mental health theory.

In the final chapters Bishop Anson Phelps Stokes, Jr., of Massachusetts will discuss the meaning of consultation for his diocese, and Bishop David E. Richards will analyze the possible impact of mental health consultation on the Church as a whole and the implications of this program for other religious denominations.

Before turning to these matters, however, I would like to take this opportunity to thank those who sponsored this book and those who provided the material on which it is based:

The Reverend Mason Wilson and the Reverend Shirley Goodwin, for much advice and information; the Reverend Thomas Bigham and Rabbi Ben Zion Gold, who reviewed parts of the manuscript; the parish clergy of Massachusetts and the consultants of the Harvard Laboratory of Community Psychiatry, who cannot be named because to do so would violate confidentiality, but without whose help this book literally could not have been written; and those who provided financial support: the American Academy of Religion and Mental Health, the Executive Council of the Episcopal Church, and the Ella Lyman Cabot Fund.

R.B.C.

Contents

*Helping
the Helpers
to Help*

chapter 1

Background
and Evolution

The mental health consultation program of the Episcopal Diocese of Massachusetts and the Harvard Laboratory of Community Psychiatry evolved during the 1960s out of requests and suggestions of clergy for some kind of resource to support them in maintaining their increasingly onerous calling. The ministers enlisted the active collaboration of their bishop, convincing him not only to sponsor such a program for them, but also to take advantage himself of the services of a psychiatric consultant to widen his own perspective on the psychological and human-relations issues that complicated his role. Throughout its history, therefore, the program has moved by the initiative of the clergy. It not only originated with them, but they negotiated and largely administered it; and its focus has thus been held to the specific and immediate needs of the men in the parishes.

The idea of creating such a program was born during a period of national ferment when the minister's role was subjected to particular strain. The civil-rights marches were taking place; President Kennedy had just been assassinated; the Vietnam War was beginning to worsen; and urban riots and widespread drug abuse were growing commonplace. These events, with their attendant violence and confusion, were ines-

3

capably the daily preoccupation of most citizens, and particularly of ministers, who sometimes found their own responses at variance with those of major segments of their congregations.

Those in parish ministry came to realize that there were more disturbed people in their communities than they had ever imagined. The times, they felt, had stimulated insecurities and anxieties that may have always lurked beneath the surface, but which had been contained in a quieter atmosphere. Now, with values in turmoil, with the "God-is-dead" theology growing popular, with violence apparently universal, clergy were startled by the number of "sick responses" that they encountered in reaction to the civil-rights struggle, the war, and drugs. As one minister recalled, "Every parish was shaken to the foundation—all the latent mental health problems seemed to surface at this time"; and the clergyman, with minimal preparation, was expected to advise and heal.

With mounting pressure on the clergy, the difficulties of their role and flaws in the administrative design of their churches were exaggerated and exposed. In Massachusetts, gadflies criticized the institutional church for being conventional and anachronistic. Theological education, they felt, was too academic and failed to prepare students for the tumultuous world in which they would work. These clergy agitated, therefore, for a reexamination of seminary curricula, and they insisted that provisions must be made for bringing alumni up to date. Furthermore, they held that since conditions continue to change, isolated doses of education or postgraduate courses would not suffice. Instead, they asked that all ministers have opportunities for periodic in-service training in the style of retooling programs offered by businesses to their executives. They were influenced in their demands by at least one model within the church, the Pastoral Institute of Washington, D.C., which offered intensive training to deacons during their first year in the ministry and postgraduate courses for older men, as well as operating as a source of referrals for those with pastoral problems.

Besides complaining of the shortcomings of their church in educating and supporting clergy, these men deplored the "superficiality" of religious life. The churches, they held, might gather members hungry for friendship and fellowship into a quiet and congenial sanctuary, but they failed to send them out again to tackle the ugly problems of the community. Contemporary religion, they believed, had shrunk from its duty to promote reform. Now, secular institutions like Business and Education had stepped into the vacuum; but these activists wanted the clergy to return to the forefront of the struggle against the weighty issues of the day.

In order for ministers to resume this role, it was clear that they needed more support than they had found in the past; for, as one man put it, by the early 1960s, "It suddenly came to light that the clergyman is one of the loneliest people in the world." In the Episcopal Church, his only support in the field was a sympathetic bishop. But the bishop, especially in a large diocese like Massachusetts, faced so many demands that he had difficulty ministering adequately to each of his priests. The natural local allies of clergy, on the whole, had failed them. Vestries and rectors were often jealous of their respective prerogatives, so that instead of supporting the clergyman, governing bodies might check his programs. Neighboring clergy were largely distrusted. Rather than turning to each other with their difficulties, ministers tended to keep up a good front and to insist to colleagues that they certainly had no problems in *their* parishes. This was a measure of insecurity and low self-esteem, as were the commonly voiced complaints about fellow priests: "Oh, you know clergy, you can never rely on them. They never answer their mail, they never return phone calls, and they are always late for meetings!"

In this atmosphere, mutual-support groups were rare. If they occurred at all, they were usually ecumenical, as though it were easier to discuss difficulties with men of other religions and denominations than with members of one's own set, with whom rivalries and personalities might too easily intrude. A few interdisciplinary groups were also formed, where ministers and medical or psychiatric personnel discussed common interests. In Massachusetts, such a group was created in 1949 at the Wellesley Human Relations Center by Dr. Erich Lindemann to study bereavement in the aftermath of Boston's Coconut Grove fire. Another existed during the 1950s and early 1960s, when six clergymen and six psychiatrists, including Dr. Clemence Benda and Ina May Greer, met every six weeks to present papers in turn on the problems of aging. The group lasted for seven or eight years; but it was characteristic of organizations like this that a few years later almost no one remembered its existence.

Despite such groups, clergy often found themselves isolated from fellow caregivers. Most ministers were not trained by their seminaries to consult with colleagues from other professions. As one man put it, "You expected the school department to ask your opinion on members of your congregation, but you never thought of asking them for any help in handling your own problem cases. Or a doctor might phone to say that one of your parishioners was dying; but you wouldn't expect to ask him for any information on the patient and his family beyond a bare diagnosis. Most ministers don't have the foggiest notion of how you consult with another person or how important that can be."

Clergy also found themselves in some measure isolated from their congregations. "In the past," observed one minister, "a clergyman called himself the servant of the community, but everyone knew that he was their leader. Now he calls himself a leader, but he and the congregation both know that he is only their servant. Everyone pays lip service to the significance of a minister's role, but everyone knows that it has moved right to the fringe of people's lives. And don't think it doesn't rankle to be nothing but the paid lackey of the man in the front pew!"

In this atmosphere, ministers tended to be swayed by the deprecatory views of some vocal laymen that they were unspecialized in an age which respected only specialization; that they lacked definable techniques for helping people which could yield objective, measurable results; that a well-planned budget was more commendable than the spiritual validity of the minister's message.

For some clergy, indeed, administrative demands offered a convenient escape from frustrations and doubts about their own religious vocation. Some became social activists, as though searching for a larger visible usefulness. Some tried psychotherapy or some other form of self-exploration, feeling that their discontent and self-doubt rose from their own irrationality. Others campaigned for institutional reforms that would raise the status of clergy, like a trade union to improve wages and working conditions, or an association to oversee professional standards. Others, however, felt uncomfortable about demanding professional rights when their vocation was to serve. They wanted to be professionalized as pastors, not as business executives or social workers.

In Massachusetts, by the early 1960s, the clergy's needs had crystallized around three areas: more education, help with handling the seemingly growing numbers of emotional problems that were brought before them, and some form of support that would raise their sense of accomplishment and self-esteem. In 1964, therefore, a group of clergy drafted a proposal which was passed by the Diocesan Convention of that year. It established a committee to study the need for such things as providing social workers for communities where there were many social problems but few local agencies, and for eventually founding a Pastoral Care Institute for Greater Boston.

After studying a list of such needs, the committee concluded that they were not as salient or feasible as had been thought. They found on examination that there was no dearth of social agencies in the community after all. On the contrary, as a consequence of the 1963 Federal Community Mental Health Act, Massachusetts was encouraging the establishment of yet more caregiving institutions throughout the Commonwealth. The committee also concluded that the diocese did not have enough money to provide social workers for parishes as had been suggested.

The committee decided against creating a Pastoral Care Institute. They saw that this would duplicate the work of the Danielsen Pastoral Counseling Center at Boston University, which already offered pastoral care on a nondenominational basis; and they felt, furthermore, that the whole idea of creating another academic setting, and the ivory-tower approach which such an institution implied, was less desirable than a new, practical, down-to-earth program which would be rooted in the parishes and in the actual problems of parishioners.

It so happened that among the members of the study committee was a young psychiatric resident at Massachusetts Mental Health Center who was a student at the Harvard Laboratory of Community Psychiatry. He described the consultation programs which the Laboratory already offered to other groups of caregivers, and recommended that the committee explore the possibility of mounting a similar service.

Professor Gerald Caplan, Director of the Laboratory, recalled the steps which led to the eventual implementation of this suggestion:

A psychiatric resident in one of my seminars came up to me one day after I had given a lecture on the place of mental health consultation in preventive psychiatry, and asked if I would advise him about some volunteer work he was doing for his church. Since I was in a hurry to get away to another meeting, and I did not feel comfortable giving my usual brief response to a student's after-class question because I imagined that the issue he was raising could not be dealt with quickly, I arranged to see him later that week for a longer chat. What he then told me so aroused my interest that I offered to meet with him for several sessions in order to help him clarify the situation in which he was involved and work out how best to put into practice in this volunteer work some of the concepts I was trying to teach him in my seminar. In effect, we agreed that I would give him occasional informal supervision over the next few months to guide his extracurricular activities.

He told me that for some years he had been an active lay worker in the Episcopal Church, and that recently he had been appointed to a diocesan planning committee charged with developing ways of helping parish priests deal with the mental health and social-welfare aspects of their duties. I was quite ignorant of the structure and operations of the Episcopal Church, but the researches of Gurin, *et al.*[1] and other studies with which I was familiar, as well as the work over many years of my friend and colleague Erich Lindemann, had long impressed me with the importance of the potential contribution of clergymen to the mental health of their parishioners. I therefore felt that if the Episcopal Church was taking active steps to develop a mental health program focused on its parish clergy, this was likely to be a significant matter for community mental health in Massachusetts. Accordingly, I devoted several sessions with the young psychiatrist to learning about the organization of his church, and to helping him understand the complex forces that were impinging on his planning committee, as well as the implications of these for his own role. I also began to feel that I wanted to know more about the actual operations of parish clergy, and to share this knowledge with my community mental health specialist students. So, I suggested that the young psychiatrist should tell the chairman of his committee, who was a friend of his and who had been responsible for inviting him to join in the planning endeavor, that he had been talking with me about these matters and that I was very interested to meet him and perhaps to invite him to come and lecture in my community mental health seminar.

It turned out, not unexpectedly, that this parson had a keen interest in community mental health, so he was pleased to come in for a talk with me; and he later lectured to my students about the mental health aspects of parish work and the psychosocial burdens and opportunities of clergymen. My students and staff, on our side, talked with him about our views concerning population-oriented psychiatry, and we told him about our attempts to spread the effects of our specialized knowledge throughout the community by offering consultation to such caregivers as public-health nurses, schoolteachers, probation officers, and general physicians. We raised the possibility of a similar approach with clergymen.

After this seminar, the rector asked me whether I would be willing to come and talk about our ideas with his committee; and naturally

I agreed, especially as the psychiatric resident also urged me to come so that I could add my authority to support his advocacy of a population approach in their planning, rather than the traditional individual-treatment projects that some of the committee members had been proposing.

During my subsequent meeting with the planning committee, I emphasized my interest in their work because of its implications for supporting ordinary people in their struggles to master life stresses which were likely to have a significant effect on their mental health; and I described our mental health consultation approach to dealing with similar issues in schools, public-health departments, and welfare agencies. I pointed out that although our work in all these settings was based on a common body of theory and methodology, each of the organizations and professions had molded the pattern of its collaboration with us to suit its own special needs and resources. I offered to work with the planning committee if it should wish to explore the development of a mental health consultation program for parish clergy. The committee members expressed great interest in such a possibility; and in response to their questions, I indicated a variety of feasible ways of organizing a program and told them how much each would cost.

Over the next few months, the planning committee continued to meet; and the psychiatric resident reported to me from time to time that the members were gradually shaping a proposal for a mental health consultation program in collaboration with our Laboratory of Community Psychiatry, and were mobilizing support for it within the decision-making units of the diocese.

By the end of the year, no clear decision had emerged; the psychiatric resident graduated from our program; and the chairman of the planning committee left the area to take a position as rector of a large parish in a distant diocese. At that stage, I would have written the matter off as an abortive attempt to start what might have been an interesting new project, except that from time to time I met the young psychiatrist at symphony concerts, and he kept telling me that although he was no longer actively involved with the committee, he knew that the issue was still under discussion, and that a new chairman had been appointed, a parish priest with much experience and interest in mental health matters.

Toward the middle of the second year, the new planning committee chairman came to see me. He brought with him the draft text of a resolution to be submitted by his committee to the forthcoming annual Diocesan Convention. This resolution proposed the establishment of a consultation program, and authorized the expenditure of the necessary funds to organize it during the next fiscal year. The chairman also told me that his committee felt that in order for the consultation program with parish clergy to be effective, it was essential that some kind of consultation should be concurrently offered to the bishop and the staff of his central office who were responsible for providing administrative, spiritual, and pastoral support to all the clergy of the diocese. I agreed that this sounded sensible, and we arranged that I should go with him and other members of his committee to discuss the matter with Bishop Anson Phelps Stokes, Jr.

That meeting was most interesting. I quickly realized that the bishop had not been kept fully informed of the deliberations of the planning committee, and that in particular he had not heard that consultation to him and his staff was to be a crucial aspect of the new program. The planning committee apparently considered this a delicate matter to raise with the bishop, since it implied that they judged his supportive efforts for the clergy of his diocese to be less than perfect. The committee had delayed dealing with this issue until I could be present; and, in fact, I found myself at the meeting playing the role of justifying this element of the program by quoting from our experience in other settings, where we had confirmed the value of offering consultation to the key administrators of an organization in order to provide the framework for consultation with line workers about psychosocial problems of their clients.

At first, Bishop Stokes was somewhat taken aback by the suggestion of his clergy that he too should receive mental health consultation. He said that he was too busy struggling with many pressing problems to be able to afford the time to talk regularly with a consultant. Also, he felt that the small budget that might be available for this program might better be used to give direct help to the parsons who were burdened by immediate and inescapable mental health problems among their parishioners. However, as the meeting continued, as I gave him more and more details about our philosophy and experience, as he began to develop a friendly relationship with me, and as he came to realize that I myself might be his consultant, he gave his tentative approval to the program, with the proviso that the details of the amount and type of my possible consultation to him and his headquarters staff should be left open for subsequent molding in the light of our joint experience. We accordingly agreed on a budget that would cover weekly consultation for two groups of parish clergy as well as headquarters consultation sessions every three or four weeks.

The plan was ratified at the Diocesan Convention, and the program started at the beginning of the next academic year, 1966–67. The parish clergy were recruited and divided into the two groups by a staff member of the central office in collaboration with the chairman of the planning committee, who made arrangements with the rectors of two centrally located churches to act as hosts. Two psychiatrists were assigned from among the Fellows of the Harvard Laboratory of Community Psychiatry to act as consultant to the groups and also to offer occasional individual consultation, on demand, to members. Professor Caplan worked out a consultation program for Bishop Stokes and his headquarters staff, and had regular meetings with the psychiatric team to coordinate and monitor their activities. These latter sessions often revealed that similar issues were weighing on both diocesan headquarters and parish congregations. Care was taken, however, not to leak such information from one level to the other, so that each consultant preserved the confidentiality of his own setting.

During the first year, everything ran smoothly. Each consultation group had about twenty members, and attendance at the weekly meetings usually averaged ten to fifteen men. Most of the consultees seemed satisfied, although there were some dropouts by spring. At the end of the year, a practice was begun which still continues: comments and suggestions were solicited from the consultants and consultees and were reported to a special evaluation meeting attended by the Laboratory staff, the bishop, and the diocesan organizing committee. At this meeting, the consultation agreement was renegotiated, and the next year's program was planned in light of this appraisal of past experience.

The following year, two groups were formed, one composed of alumni from both groups of the previous season, and the second made up of new members. In addition, a third group was started for the wives of some of the men in the program. Attendance was fairly regular, and the level of participation high, although the groups had to adjust to a new set of consultants whose personalities and styles differed from those of their predecessors.

In the third year, two groups were again set up, but they met less often. At the end, when questions were raised about whether the diocese could afford to continue funding the program, the men offered to pay for the sessions themselves.

During the fourth year, the program underwent a crisis. Bishop Stokes retired, and after the consecration of his successor, Bishop John M. Burgess, the diocesan staff was reshuffled. The men who had created and maintained the program were replaced by others. A new administrator was appointed with responsibility for centralizing administrative tasks so as to free the bishop as much as possible for pastoral duties and organizational leadership. One effect of this was that consultation was taken out of the hands of the two men who had been running it since its inception, the staff man at diocesan headquarters and the parish priest who had been chairman of the original planning committee. It was reclassified as one form of Career Development, and was assigned to a newly established committee that tried to reorganize it in accordance with the results of a survey designed to poll the interests of clergymen in the career-development field. Unfortunately, by the time this survey had been completed and its results analyzed, the year was well advanced; and the parish clergy had been confused by the meaning of the survey, which few associated with consultation.

Bishop Burgess wanted to continue the program, and he began to consult regularly with Dr. Caplan. But his new administrator, who had come from another diocese, never understood it, and kept trying to conceptualize it as part of his career-development approach that was derived from personnel practices in business.

The consultation program began to flounder and nearly died amid executive confusion. Two psychiatric consultants met as co-leaders of a single group of three to six parish clergy. The Laboratory was tempted to end the project because it

seemed a squandering of resources. The two consultants, however, urged Dr. Caplan not to stop a program that they found
so interesting and from which the few members of the group
were clearly benefiting. And they felt that the Laboratory
should not abandon a learning experience that was so valuable for the Laboratory Fellows, a group of experienced mental health workers who spend a year in specialized studies of
community mental health theory and methodology. Further,
Bishop Burgess wanted the program to continue, having been
asked by many clergy who had participated in previous years
to intervene and revive it.

Accordingly, the Laboratory decided to try again. Dr. Caplan arranged with Bishop Burgess that they personally organize the consultation program the following year. They drafted
a letter to all parish clergy inviting them to participate in one
of two weekly consultation groups; and the bishop received
about fifty positive replies.

During the fifth year, 1971–72, the average attendance at
each group returned to fifteen. Bishop Burgess went to a number of sessions, thus demonstrating that consultation is a supportive service to the clergy from their bishop, acting as a
bridge between headquarters and line workers. The clergymen
could now see that the bishop himself was directly involved in
their welfare, rather than dealing with them through intermediaries.

The survival of this program depended in large measure on
the fact that the clergy molded it and, except for a brief inter-
lude, operated it and made it their property. Thus it came
from the grass roots, and it remained focused on the actual
needs of parish clergy. Furthermore, at every stage of the program, from that of preliminary negotiations, through the establishment of a partnership between the diocese and the Laboratory, and as the program was renewed year after year, long
after the two institutions had come to know and trust each
other, every aspect of organization was periodically evaluated

and renegotiated. Understanding and accord were never taken for granted. Terminology was carefully defined, and formal working agreements were redrawn each year, spelling out the mutual expectations of both sides so that both parties might be satisfied as much as possible and the ground rules would be so defined ahead of time that neither party would be surprised.

A third factor which may have contributed to a climate hospitable to consultation was the existence of another program that began at about the same time at the Episcopal Theological Seminary for training parish clergy to act as supervisors for students in field placements. Many of those engaged in the Laboratory's consultation program were simultaneously studying this new skill at the Seminary. Their supervision classes were taught by a social worker, who in the course of her lectures, frequently spoke of how she herself regularly asked for consultation on complicated cases from psychiatrists. She thus became a model for the clergymen of a highly skilled professional who maintained continuing and regular relations with members of a different discipline in the community. They now realized that they did not have to handle each case alone, or else unload it onto another agency or specialist. Instead, they came to see that they might cope with a wider range of parishioners if they were able to enlist the cooperation and advice of workers in other fields.

Finally, both the clergy and the Laboratory consultants were highly motivated. The clergy needed the education and support which they found in the program. The Laboratory, as a community mental health facility, was eager to increase the ministers' awareness of, and proficiency in, their own specialized role. This role, as we will see in the next chapter, has the potential for playing a significant part in promoting mental health in the parishes.

chapter 2

The Clergyman as Community Mental Health Worker

One of the dilemmas shared by many clergymen is that of defining their own professional identity. In this secular age, men of religion have come to wonder whether their ministry has any effect on their people's welfare. Particularly in their counseling of troubled parishioners, clergy find themselves without the formal technology of other helping professions. They do not have codified procedures which can be clearly taught, tested, and certified like those of a clinician. There seems to be less precision in what ministers do. Their actions in any given case are determined, they fear, not by objective precepts but by intuition, experience, or personal wisdom and by the application of abstract religious edicts framed hundreds or thousands of years earlier. Clergymen often pine for the security which they imagine that other professionals have, which comes from the capacity to measure with certainty the effect of their actions. This self-doubt is often sharpened by the concurrence of laymen who question the competence of a minister to counsel disturbed parishioners without benefit of specialized psychiatric training and degrees.

Doubt has led many clergy to denigrate the qualities of their own role and to hanker after the ways of other disciplines. Just as in the organization of their parish or congregational affairs where many have adopted the management techniques of business, so in counseling, some of the most concerned ministers have tried to copy the values and methods of another field—that of mental health workers. Here the psychiatrist is seen as the supreme model, since he is regarded as physician to the whole man, unlike other specialists who appear to deal with physical or social fragments outside the unified human context.

This evaluation of psychiatrists as ideal counselors has had a sad effect on the identity of the clergy. It has led many to pick up the superficialities of psychiatric practice, like the fifty-minute hour, at the expense of their own more flexible style of apportioning time to those who ask their help. It has led some to wander out of their depth into intra-psychic analysis without the years of training and supervision which help to guarantee a psychiatric patient's safety. It has turned a few into excellent therapists, but has thereby removed them from the normative role of clergymen. Most damaging, it has led many ministers to adopt as their preferred model in helping the disturbed an ideology which some leading psychiatrists had discarded years ago. The exclusive reliance on an individual, intra-psychic, long-term, depth model of psychotherapy is regarded by many mental health workers as archaic, although some ministers feel they are giving better care the closer they approach it. On the other hand, the focus that certain progressive psychiatrists are now working toward is not only very different, it is, paradoxically, strikingly like that contained within the natural heritage of the traditional clergyman.

The clergy, because of the customs of their discipline, have certain innate advantages in dealing with human problems. The extent to which these exist in any particular denomination or the ease with which any individual minister can handle them varies. Nevertheless, these tools of a traditional religious counselor can all be developed and spread if they are sufficiently valued.

In the first place, clergymen have a responsibility acknowledged both by themselves and by their congregations to care for everybody in their flock. They have, in other words, a population focus in much of their organizational and liturgical work which, if extended to their counseling functions, could significantly increase their helpfulness. Community psychiatry has only recently won recognition for the principle that mental illness is more effectively contained if clinicians concentrate not merely on single patients in their offices and treatment institutions, but on a total population within a bounded community. Inside these borders, which may be geographical or institutional—as in the army, or a school system, or a church —caregivers are responsible for the mental health needs of the entire population, both sick and well. They are required not only to treat existing cases; to help safeguard certain groups within the population found to be at special risk; and to aid those who have recovered from mental disturbances to reenter their social and occupational networks, but they are also responsible for helping those individuals who may never suffer psychiatric disturbances, but who, in the course of the normal vicissitudes of life, encounter stresses which temporarily upset their emotional equilibrium.

So community mental health workers are preoccupied not so fully with individuals as with families, neighborhoods, and institutions—with the complex social systems that largely determine any person's state of well-being. By focusing on these larger units, they seek to enhance the development of widespread supportive structures so that the inhabitants of areas slated for urban renewal, or students facing major examinations, or widows with young children are not taxed beyond their strength.

It is well to realize how many natural advantages a clergyman has if he is prepared to consider his counseling role within a community framework—advantages which mental health workers can develop only with the greatest difficulty, if at all.

In the first place, the clergyman is known by his population and he knows them. Unlike many psychiatric caregivers, the minister is not largely invisible and, therefore, invested by those he seeks to help with fearsome characteristics which the client must fight before he dares to approach the mental health worker. The minister is widely known; and the fact that he may be regarded with some awe as a man of God makes him seem powerful, but not necessarily frightening.

The ease with which a person approaches a minister is also increased by the fact that in doing so he does not label himself a "case." There is no stigma in his own eyes or in those of others if he contacts a clergyman, whereas there may well be one if he goes instead to the local mental health center. In order to bypass this very problem, mental health professionals and their colleagues in other caregiving fields now favor the development of comprehensive, multiservice centers to which any member of the community may apply. The client may define his concern as medical, legal, vocational, educational, or psychiatric—and all these services are available on the premises. But whatever the individual gives as his reason for coming— that he needs vocational guidance because of trouble with his job, or he needs further education, or he needs treatment for alcoholism—he can receive help as needed in other categories without committing himself to being a psychiatric, or a medical, or an illiteracy case.

All of this effort to disengage the help of mental health workers from the shame that is often associated with it requires ingenious planning by mental health personnel, whereas clergymen have the ideal situation by right because of the popular image of their role. This means that in their efforts to redefine their counseling functions in order to bring them closer to those of prestigious psychiatrists, clergymen are apt to limit their parishioners' freedom in approaching them. Their offers of help will be in danger of rousing the same fear and embarrassment as do those of mental health workers.

Because the individual who seeks help from a minister has less inhibitions to overcome before coming to him, the clergy tend to see people at an early stage of disturbance when the chance of recovery is at its height. Ministers see cases in crisis. At this acute moment of upset, people are unusually susceptible to help, and that help means far more to the individual's future mental health than it would after time has elapsed and some degree of balance has been reestablished in his personality. One of the most economical and effective ways of reducing disturbance in a population may well be to reach people at such pivotal moments when a relatively small amount of counsel and support can make a major difference to that individual's future life.

Most mental health agencies are at a disadvantage here because by the time they see many of their cases, this critical moment has passed. It then takes much more time, effort, and specialized techniques to achieve the ends that might have been won so much more easily if the case could have been seen while it was fresh. The minister, however, has ready access in this critical period. Not only do people call him in sooner, but he is often present anyway at sickbeds, deathbeds, and other crisis points.

Moreover, the clergyman is often sufficiently master of his time that he can reach someone in acute distress within hours or even minutes if necessary, unlike other caregivers who have more difficulty scheduling appointments. We have been impressed in the consultation groups by the number of ministers who report not only answering an anguished phone call with a home visit within a short time, but also with the way in which, after assessing the situation, they can spend two, three, or even five hours containing a threatened explosion. After such intensive and prompt infusions of support, it is instructive to note how quickly a parishioner returns to independence and normal functioning; whereas denying him such lavish help in a crisis often creates a need for long-term care.

The speed and efficacy with which a clergyman can answer a call for help is also increased by the knowledge about members of his congregation that he has accumulated over years; for the minister, like the vanishing but now sadly missed general practitioner, knows his population more intimately than does any other category of caregivers. A minister sees his people continuously, both in their normal state and when they are in need. This knowledge allows him to approach the problem brought to him more directly, without spending so much time and effort laying groundwork and establishing relationships in early phases of counseling as a mental health worker must.

Knowledge of his population also allows a minister to assess the seriousness of a parishioner's predicament more rapidly, since he is already equipped with earlier observations of the individual's temperament and background. One of the men in a consultation group, for example, alluded to a call he had recently received from a level-headed, mature sixteen-year-old girl who got on well with her parents, to say that she had been forced into disobeying them seriously and had to see the minister at once. The clergyman, because of his close contacts with the family, realized that this was highly peculiar; and when he drove up to his parishioner's house a quarter of an hour later, he found that his fears were unfortunately justified. The girl's parents had suddenly learned of her secret engagement to a black and had reacted with an ultimatum—either she give the man up or leave home. Had the minister not known the family, as would have been the case with most other caregivers to whom the girl might have appealed, he might have concluded that this was an ordinary confrontation between parents and an adolescent, and might have treated the call with less urgency than it in fact required.

Another aspect of a minister's availability is the fact that he is usually not paid by the individuals who come for help, but instead receives a salary from the community. It may not be too fanciful to compare this situation to the latest projected reform in medical and psychiatric care which seeks to improve the delivery of service to a population through prepaid insurance schemes. These give any member a right to obtain care, no matter how slender his means. Clergymen, however, fit into the most sophisticated of these plans, since they are rewarded for keeping people healthy, not for treating the sick. A conventional insurance plan pays for extraction of teeth, not for prophylaxis or fillings. This rewards bad preventive care. An improved plan would encourage doctors to keep patients well and to avoid unnecessary surgery and hospitalization. Similarly, a minister is not paid extra for counseling those severely disturbed for long periods; but if he keeps his people healthy, he is rewarded with fewer demands on his time, so his concern with preventive programs should be greater.

One of the major advantages that a clergyman has, which is shared by no other profession, is his recognized license to intervene in the lives of his congregation. He does not have to obtain special sanction to do so, nor does he have to worry about trespassing on the territory of other professionals who may be acting already in the case. He is entitled to maintain surveillance over the welfare of any member of his flock, and he may mobilize the friends and relatives of a troubled individual without most people accusing him of interference.

An example of this was cited at a consultation session. A wife came to the minister with an account of her husband's infidelity. This clergyman had learned over several years of consultation to consider such problems within the context of systems rather than as a matter exclusively for individual counseling. In addition to counseling the wife, therefore, the clergyman summoned on various occasions and in differing combinations the husband, the couple's teenage son, the other woman, the other woman's family, and a neighbor in whom some of the parties confided. After interviewing and advising them, the minister dispatched these people to community counseling services and then checked back to see if they were being helped. He spoke to the guidance center's staff and redeployed the helping agents. He learned that some of the people were making fun of the agency's advice after their sessions, and he called on them to take a more mature attitude. Despite the fact that some of those involved were not even members of his parish, while others were not regular churchgoers, none questioned his right to enter their lives on his own initiative; on the contrary, they were only too relieved to find so effective a source of counseling and so efficient a mobilizer and coordinator of other social agencies. The local guidance-center staff were also grateful for his advice and for the discipline maintained among those he had sent. The minister admitted that it had been a hectic case, but one in which a focus on systems, as well as on individuals, had made a major difference to the outcome.

Access to parishioners is increased further by the custom, found in a number of denominations, of ministers making home visits. Some clergy give priority in their house calls to those who appear troubled or withdrawn and who are thereby provided an opportunity to confide in the minister earlier than they might have done on their own initiative. Some clergy, however, dislike this custom, regarding it as antiquated and a waste of time, since they may find an empty house or a cool reception when they call. They also feel that such visits tend to "deteriorate" into social occasions, devoid of serious content. Those who use this method effectively, however, do not minimize the value of "mere" social interaction. They regard a chat over coffee as a way of maintaining a parishioner's identification with the community, and of preserving an atmosphere in which more critical contacts can be readily made whenever necessary. They also find that phoning ahead helps to prevent wasted journeys.

Unlike mental health workers, clergymen may be able to remain close to those they have once counseled. The role of a minister is often so perceived by laymen that members of his congregation are usually able to confide intimate details of their lives to him, and then face him socially afterward. There is a generally held opinion that people can confess private feelings to a minister, even among groups which do not have formal confession. They expect that since he is so accustomed to observing the vagaries of human nature he will not be shocked by such revelations, and will not allow them to prejudice his normal relationship with the individual. This, of course, varies with the personality of the individual minister and with the conventions of his denomination. There are clergy who are readily outraged, who are so preoccupied with denouncing sin that they fail to understand the pain that often gives rise to and accompanies forbidden acts. Their rigidity and censoriousness make those in trouble hesitate to approach them. But there is also an increasing number of ministers who, while remaining loyal to their ideals, nevertheless differentiate Sin from a sinner. They can listen to their parishioners' accounts of sordid feelings and actions without shock and without rejecting them; and they can comfort those caught in all-too-human predicaments, even while deploring the errors that they have committed. Many of these religious leaders feel that while retaining their moral sense of right and wrong, they need never, in consequence, reject or fail to understand and welcome those who transgress the standards which their religions uphold.

Clergymen who are themselves easy in this confessional situation can convince even those laymen who might hesitate to accept it. In the words of one highly experienced minister: "When people come to me for counsel and seem a bit squeamish, I tell them that they can regard me as a bottomless pit. Information drops in and disappears unless they want to discuss it again. So when I meet them in the street the next day, they don't need to feel embarrassed, because I'm certainly thinking of something quite other than their disclosures." In such a situation, the minister's opportunity to follow the aftermath of a crisis and to guard against future eruptions in the individual's emotional or social life is much greater than that of other caregivers.

The minister's ability to offer intermittent care over long periods of time is strengthened by the fact that, unlike a clinician, he is not bound by a treatment model that decrees that each case must have a beginning and an end, after which the caregiver and his patient must part. The clergyman does not have to terminate a relationship in this way. He remains a source of security to people who know that he will always be there when needed without the intervening obstacle of a new sortie through referral systems and intake procedures.

The minister's opportunity to maintain contact with cases is enhanced further by his ability to apportion time more flexibly. Since he is not tied to a fifty-minute hour in his own office, he is able not only to devote large blocks of time to people at acute stages of a crisis, but he can also support chronic and lonely cases through short, regular meetings. What many widows, for example, are grateful for is a clergyman who drops in for a cup of tea every few weeks to ask how things are.

There was a case of a minister in a rural area who, for many years, went regularly to visit a lady parishioner every week for half an hour or so. They chatted about local affairs; and since the lady always seemed preoccupied by worries about her neighbors slighting her, the clergyman generally found himself reassuring his hostess that people thought well of her and that she might have misunderstood the comments she overheard and took to heart in the grocery shop. While attending a mental health conference, the minister told a psychiatrist about his parishioner. The doctor concluded from several things the minister said that the lady was schizophrenic and that the minister had been maintaining her in an active life for years with little expenditure of time and effort, but with a great deal of kindness. Unhappily, however, the clergyman was horrified by this revelation. Not only did this psychiatric label invest his old friend with terrifying associations of raving madness, but he felt that as a minister he was not competent to deal with schizophrenia. The fact that he had succeeded with the woman for years, and had gently reasoned her out of countless paranoid delusions, did not prevent him from never going near her again.

This sad story illustrates the danger of clergymen equating formal training with skill, and their propensity for avoiding cases that they could handle competently, only because a label has been applied to the sufferer which makes him sound too fragile or dangerous to be managed by anyone but a specialist. That would be all very well if there were enough specialists to treat all cases, but unfortunately there are so few that only 10 to 20 percent of the disturbed ever reach mental health services. So for many, like that schizophrenic lady who lived far from enlightened psychotherapists, the choice may be between no psychiatric care at all and the qualitatively different, but by no means inferior, style of help offered by ministers.

Clergymen, therefore, have natural advantages in their ready access to disturbed members of the population and in obtaining sanction to intervene in their lives. In the content of their counseling, they have also inherited functions which are often as effective as those of psychotherapists.

As one reads about ways of dealing with mental illness over the centuries, and as one sees cases of disturbance which have cleared without recourse to psychiatrists, one realizes that while specialist mental health workers may be successful in dealing with many of their patients, they cannot claim an exclusive power to cure mental disorder. On the contrary, their style is one among many that have evolved over centuries to combat human misery. While it may be highly potent in helping some people, it may be less effective with others; and there is not even proof that those who are thus aided could not have made an equally certain recovery if their problems had been approached from a quite different angle, as requiring a change of job, for example, or a strict diet and exercise, to cite popular remedies from the past. Clergymen were always recognized throughout history as having unusual powers in managing mental illness, even after the belief that madness was demonic possession had been routed by the scientific rationalism of the eighteenth and nineteenth centuries. It is conceivable, then, that the role still enables men to minister effectively to such cases.

It is known that social influences can alter the severity of even those mental conditions that are organically determined. Many psychiatrists, for example, agree that stimulation by contact with other human beings can slow deterioration in cases of senility and arteriosclerosis. The capacities of retarded or brain-damaged children can be much improved by the concern of, and interaction with, others. And mental health clinicians in the army have found that combat neurosis can best be treated by returning a soldier to his unit as soon as possible. In the seventeenth century, Robert Burton, in the *Anatomy of Melancholy*, warned those whom we would now call neurotics never to be idle or alone. Dr. Samuel Johnson, a life-long sufferer from irrational fears and guilt, dreaded solitude, when he became the prey of his imagination; for, he wrote, "in solitude, perplexity swells into distraction and grief settles into melancholy." [1] On the same theme, he wrote to his friend Mrs. Thrale, who with her husband had won his passionate gratitude for rescuing him out of the midst of an acute attack of his disorder and had established him in their own lively household, that solitude "is dangerous to reason, without being favorable to virtue. . . . Remember that the solitary mortal is certainly luxurious, probably superstitious, and possibly mad; the mind stagnates for want of employment, grows morbid and is extinguished like a candle in foul air." Another sufferer, Laurence Sterne, the eighteenth-century novelist who was also a parish priest in the Church of England, wrote: "Yet still, it is not good for a man to be alone. . . . Give me some companion in my journey, be it only to remark to, How our shadows lengthen as the sun goes down:—to whom I may say, How fresh is the face of nature! How sweet the flowers of the field! How delicious are these fruits!" [2]

The clergyman can reduce the isolation of disturbed parishioners by showing his own interest and by mobilizing family, neighbors, and community groups. As the leader of his congregation, he may have within his purview a variety of groups and individuals only too eager to help others—to visit the sick, or to welcome newcomers to town—for whom such work is also mentally therapeutic. Societies may be formed for members who are themselves in difficulties, to both support their own people and to incorporate new casualties. Such a fellowship, for example, was created in one church by recently bereaved members of the congregation to comfort each other and to pray for the dead; and they became an invaluable resource to which the pastor could refer other bereaved. By his own efforts and by orchestrating those of a variety of helpful agents—Ladies' Aid Societies, self-help groups, or individual professionals willing to donate their services to recipients designated by the church—a minister can combat loneliness not only among those who are naturally condemned to solitude, like old, bedridden people, handicapped children, or widows and widowers; but, like the clergyman of the schizophrenic lady mentioned earlier, he can stimulate even those with psychoses to keep as much of a hold as possible on reality by intruding social demands and concern on their alienating fantasies.

While it could not be said that insanity is a condition entered into voluntarily, nevertheless, even significantly disturbed people can be made to behave sanely if those around them insist. It was long accepted in seventeenth-, eighteenth-, and early-nineteenth-century literature on mental disorder, and is now being tested again in some psychiatric centers, that if disturbed people are shown that those around them expect them to behave like normal human beings, instead of concurring in their irrationality by accepting that they cannot help their actions because they are sick, striking improvements in behavior are likely to occur. The H. Douglas Singer Zone Center in Rockford, Illinois, under the directorship of Dr. Norris Hansell, recently produced a film, *Come Out, Come Out, Whoever You Are,*[3] that records how a group of backward, "hopeless" cases were returned to independent functioning by the educational pressure of the center staff. One of these patients had been mute for twenty years because of catatonic schizophrenia. The film shows how, under the pressure of group expectations, the man began to speak again.

Clergymen, more than psychiatrists, are authority figures, and they are in a particularly strong position to enforce normal behavior and reality-based reactions on those who temporarily lose control. Thus one minister pulled one of his parishioners out of an acute anxiety state by saying firmly, "Now, Mary, buck up!" He later told us with some awe, "You know, she did!" Another clergyman had a parishioner who was subject to occasional psychotic episodes during which he would threaten to expose himself. The man was taken to a local psychiatric clinic, where his symptoms were treated with tolerance. He cheerfully went around to all the secretaries and young social workers offering to show them his "hairy penis." It was the minister who finally dealt with the situation by firmly telling his parishioner that his language and actions were completely unacceptable and that he was to start behaving himself at once. The man, with the utmost meekness, complied despite his illness. And soon, since he was no longer acting in a "crazy way," he was sent home, where the expectation that he was now ready for normal responsibilities and pursuits helped to make him so.

In this area, the minister, the father-figure of the community, the representative of traditions which demand that man rise above his animal nature, can be the prop for weak-willed people who come to him for counsel. Some clergy, influenced by psychoanalytic practice and by the nondirective style of counseling advocated by Carl Rogers, refuse to use this authority when parishioners ask the minister to direct them in a question of morality or social responsibility. Although many clergymen are prepared to give judgments from the pulpit, some have told us that they refuse to do so in individual counseling. They feel that such a use of authority would both foster dependency in the parishioner and inhibit other laymen from appealing for help since they might fear censure. And since there is a history of authoritarianism among the clergy of some denominations, there is often emphatic rejection of anything that smacks of this style among progressive and humane ministers.

One suspects, however, that the pendulum may have swung too far, and that authoritarianism and legitimate authority have been confused. In this area, some ministers tend to forget flexibility—the fact that they can select from a range of counseling styles to suit each case. Thus a display of firm authority might fit the needs of certain individuals—like adolescents, for example—though it might be inappropriate for others. This may seem self-evident, but it is surprising how often ministers treat this issue absolutely, saying flatly that they refuse to make any decisions for any of their parishioners. They forget, one suspects, that the very fact that a layman appeals to a man of religion to ask, "Can I continue to commit adultery?" means that he has all but decided already that the answer is "No," and is asking for support in containing the instincts that he himself knows to be wrong. In the same way, many ministers are plagued by drunken or psychotic telephone callers, who ring at the most inopportune hours and threaten to damage themselves or to attack members of their family. If they intended, unambiguously, to act violently, they would do so; they would be unlikely to ask a clergyman to react first. Some of these sufferers also seem to be crying for a firm stand on the side of reason and control to counteract the overwhelming urge toward license.

In certain situations, direct orders from a clergyman may avert disaster. One such case was mentioned by a parishioner, a woman who, years before, had been in the throes of a divorce and had decided to commit suicide. She went to her clergyman, an old friend, to dare him to stop her. The minister, a normally quiet man, with no hesitation pounded on his desk and shouted, "No! You must not! God forbids it! If you do that, you will go straight to hell, and all my prayers wouldn't get you out. Are you prepared for that?" The shaken woman agreed that perhaps psychoanalysis might be a safer alternative; and twenty years later, she spoke of this minister with the most profound gratitude. Had he been less forceful in his reaction, she felt she might not have lived to do so.

Some highly sophisticated ministers have been able to use authority to obtain results in a case without provoking an examination by the parishioner of deep-rooted, complex emotions. Had these emotions been confronted directly, they would have required more time and specialized training than was available to these clergymen in order to resolve them adequately. Clergy, in this way, have been able to help people, for example, to interrupt a vicious circle which the parishioners themselves cannot see. Thus a college chaplain was appealed to by a student who, he learned, hated her mother so intensely that she could not act in any way that she imagined might inadvertently please her mother, and she was crippling her own life in consequence. The student was on the point of leaving for graduate studies abroad, but first had to go home to say goodbye to her family; and the prospect of a week with her mother was terrifying.

The chaplain immediately realized that the student's feelings were so deep-rooted that to unravel their complexity in the time that was left before the girl's departure was clearly impossible. Since he could not attack the problem from the bottom, he started at the top. He first set about showing the student what her mother must be feeling; and he succeeded in gradually turning a grotesque stereotype into a disappointed, irritable middle-aged woman who had lost the trust of her daughter. Eventually the girl agreed that she could accept the chaplain's picture intellectually, but not emotionally—she still hated her mother. The chaplain said, "I understand that, but I'm not interested in your feelings at the moment. They're irrelevant. We have very little time before you leave, and we must act. However you feel when you go home, do only what I tell you. Pretend that you are acting a part; pretend that you are a nurse with a difficult patient. Pretend anything you like, but do what I say." He then gave the girl instructions on how to act in a variety of situations where friction had always been generated in the past.

A week later, the student phoned the chaplain. She had obeyed his orders, and to her amazement something had changed. Once the vicious circle by which the two women had aggravated each other had been interrupted by the minister's warning to the girl not to respond to provocative cues, they had been able to see each other in a different light; and, as a result of the week's contact, the possibility of a healthier relationship was born.

The chaplain, as a sophisticated observer, had easily seen the vicious circle which was invisible to the mother and daughter caught in it. He wasted no time trying to explain the dynamics of the situation or trying to uncover or alter the student's tangled feelings. Instead, he gave orders which the girl could carry out with a minimum of emotional involvement. Indeed, he urged a disengaging of feelings and the playing of a part. As a result, direct experience shook the mutual stereotypes of the women, and movement was allowed in a hitherto impacted situation while all the forces by which they defended and maintained their hostility were off guard.

Some men have found that, because of the lower concern with religion among many of their parishioners, they need fear less now than formerly the effects of taking an authoritative stand. Thus, if the minister's advice does not suit an individual, the layman is apt to discount it, which he would be less likely to do with the advice of a specialist clinician to whom he has paid a fee. This may mean that a clergyman can do less harm with bad advice than a mental health worker. It also seems, from the experience of some ministers, that when parishioners reject their advice, they do not necessarily reject the clergyman. Instead, they may return for another suggestion. A rabbi, for example, told a young man to take certain steps to resolve a conflict with his parents. The man returned a few days later to say that he had not taken the rabbi's advice, but that he wanted to talk to him again, since the situation at home was deteriorating. The rabbi was irritated, but also relieved that he still had an opportunity to lower the tension of the case.

Clergymen are often better able than clinicians to handle problems of guilt, long recognized as lying at the source of many disturbances, for they have the power of invoking absolution and of suggesting with the voice of authority constructive acts of contrition and steps that will exculpate the real or imagined sin. The importance of a minister's role in cases where guilt predominates was recognized in the late eighteenth and early nineteenth centuries, a time of humane and progressive reform in the care of the insane. Mental hospitals were urged by the psychiatric leaders of the day to put chaplains on their staff, not only to conduct religious services, but to counsel and treat those cases for whom guilt appeared to be the central issue of their disturbance.[4]

Because ministers testify to an eternal scheme, they can manage incurable and long-term conditions more satisfactorily than psychiatrists can. They can offer hope for eventual deliverance, and they can give a positive meaning to what may otherwise seem tragically absurd. The psychiatric model implies that if one digs deeply enough into the personality, and thereby uncovers and resolves more and more conflicts, the patient will eventually rid himself of crippling fantasies and will recover. But, as Dr. Johnson wrote in the *Rambler* (32), "The cure for the greatest part of human miseries is not radical, but palliative." Often these miseries are not susceptible to cure by analysis because they are based not on fantasies, but on harsh reality, like a marriage in which one partner is chronically frustrated, or a fatal illness. Here the clergyman is particularly helpful in promoting active resignation that allows life and dignity to continue despite crushing burdens.

Clergymen also have an advantage over the clinicians precisely because, in the mental health area, they are not professionalized, but have the flexibility of a gifted amateur. Most mental health workers see cases as belonging to categories, thus triggering the somewhat stereotyped response of "correct treatment." Clergymen, on the other hand, seem to regard cases as idiosyncratic human beings, and tailor their help to fit the specific needs of the client. Consequently, they have a greater stimulus to find unexpected, innovative approaches which often satisfy the needs of their parishioners more fully than the "correct" professional treatment. A minister told us rather apologetically of an encounter he had had with an alcoholic, in which, he said, he had "broken all the rules." A young woman appeared on his doorstep one morning, much the worse for wear, to beg for money to buy herself another drink. The minister did not argue; he gave her what she asked for. A few days later, the girl returned and the clergyman began to make friends with her. He discovered that she had tried to give up drinking on several occasions and had, from time to time, joined Alcoholics Anonymous, but she had always relapsed. She had joined a confirmation class when she was trying to reform, but at the thought of the wine at communion she became so anxious that her resolve to stay sober would not survive the taking of the sacrament, that she rushed to the local bar to calm down again. The minister encouraged the woman to try again; and this time, he persuaded her to regard communion as a way of renewing her pledge to remain sober. This happened, the minister told us, fifteen years ago; and with his help the woman has led a normal life ever since.

This raises a further point: the role of regular religious observance in preserving mental health. It has been observed that the discipline of reciting a liturgy and of carrying out formalized acts at regular intervals imposes an order on an individual's life that is of continuing therapeutic value. The fact that such observances are repeated at regular intervals steadily reinforces the message of discipline, structure, and identity. It regularly renews community contacts and devotion to that group's ideals by repeated exposure to signs of fellowship. As behavioral scientists have discovered, people need a *constant* flow of physical and social supplies and stimulation to maintain their well-being. One dose has only a limited effect; and a personality disintegrates rapidly if there is no opportunity for continuing contact with outside supports. Some people realize this instinctively. A clergyman, for example, told of a brilliant but vague mathematician who was the most scrupulous observer of religious discipline that he had ever encountered. He was startled, therefore, to discover in casual conversation that the man was an atheist. "Why," asked the minister, "are you so careful to carry out all these rules if you don't believe in God?" "It keeps me sane," the parishioner answered. "Without rules to live by, I'd get lost."

From the foregoing points, therefore, it should be seen that the diffidence of many clergymen about the value and efficacy of their own role in helping troubled people is misplaced. It is precisely by concentrating on their own traditional functions and in developing them that ministers can make a major contribution toward containing suffering in their communities. Aping the ways of other professionals, on the other hand, will only lead to loss of a valuable discipline. The clergy, in other words, should beware of selling their birthright for a mess of potage. "I may only be a piccolo, not a great trumpet," said a rabbi, "but if I give up my piccolo to play a trumpet, the orchestra will suffer for the loss of my part. I am needed too, however insignificant some people think my contribution is. I know that I help some of those who come to me, and that gives me satisfaction."

All of this, however, is not to say that mental health professionals have nothing to offer the clergy. As we will see next when we turn to a detailed discussion of mental health consultation, psychiatrists and their colleagues in psychology and social work can extend the awareness of ministers in many specialized areas so that the clergy *as clergy*, not as quasi-psychiatrists, can carry out the demands of their role with greater effectiveness and insight.

chapter 3

Mental Health Consultation*

In the seventeenth century, Robert Burton, himself a cleric, wrote in *The Anatomy of Melancholy* that the treatment of emotional illness is "as much appertaining to a divine as to a physician, and who knows not what an agreement there is between these two professions? . . . A divine in this compound mixed malady can do little alone, a physician in some kind of melancholy much less, both make an absolute cure." [1]

While nowadays we might hesitate to speak so confidently of "absolute" cures, nevertheless, certain contemporary forms of collaboration between clinicians and clergy have indeed proved mutually satisfying to members of both professions and have benefited disturbed people in the community. One of these, which seeks to serve the needs of both disciplines simultaneously, is *mental health consultation*. It enables a clergyman *consultee* to call in a specialist *consultant* to advise him on difficulties which the consultee is having in managing one of his own cases. A minister, for example, might request the help of a mental health specialist if he suspected that emotional pathology or interpersonal tensions in his parishioner or in the parishioner's family were frustrating his own efforts to ease the

* The framework for this chapter is drawn from Gerald Caplan's *The Theory and Practice of Mental Health Consultation*, Basic Books, Inc., New York, 1971, to which the reader is urged to refer for a more detailed treatment of the technical material.

37

situation. The consultant would then try to clarify these issues in the parishioner's life, for the clergyman, with two goals in mind: first, to help the minister to return to the case better able to satisfy that parishioner's needs; and, second, to enable the consultee, as a result of his experiences with this case, to gain sufficient knowledge, skill, and objectivity to handle similar situations in the future on his own.

Many mental health clinicians regard consultation to clergy and other caregivers, such as public-health nurses, general practitioners, teachers, and police, as the pivot of their own community work. This was recognized by the framers of the Federal Community Mental Health Act of 1963, who made the funding of a mental health facility depend in part on whether its staff offered consultation to other groups of professionals serving the public.

There is a ready reason for this emphasis. The professional goal of community mental health specialists is to prevent or attenuate the severity of mental suffering in the population. Since there are far too few clinicians to accomplish this task alone, they must mobilize the efforts of other caregivers by convincing them that while they are doing their own jobs, they can also help mental health personnel to do theirs. Thus nurses, physicians, police, teachers, and clergy could help to reduce emotional strain among a large number of people because their daily work naturally brings them into contact with a wide range of individuals throughout the population who are undergoing critical, and hence unbalancing, experiences. By supporting people during such crises, and by rapidly identifying those who are buckling under stress, these caregivers can prevent disturbances, or can route vulnerable cases to psychiatric first aid sooner than these clients might go on their own initiative. Consultation, therefore, has been conceived of as a medium through which community mental health specialists can spread the information and support that will enable other professionals to operate more competently and surely in this complicated area.

Consultation differs from other forms of collaboration between professionals because its primary goal is education. This focus relieves the consultant of the responsibility, axiomatic in more traditional forms of professional collaboration, for diagnosing and treating his consultee's clients. For if the consultant were only to accept every problem case into the already overburdened psychiatric network, he would never move any further toward multiplying mental health resources among other community caregivers. If he were to attempt to diagnose and treat each case himself, he would rapidly fill his time with a small number of cases, some of whom might be equally helped by nonpsychiatric interventions, thus restricting his own specialized knowledge to a relatively limited context. He would have little time left to educate other community workers to greater self-sufficiency in dealing with the vast range of mental health issues with which they are confronted daily in the community.

Consultation, therefore, is an aid to efficiency. It allows a limited number of clinicians to be deployed so that they can make the largest possible contribution to the mental health of the population. It also helps other caregivers, like ministers, to use *their* limited time for more effective relief of emotional suffering.

On the other hand, great effort is made by mental health consultants to avoid turning members of other professions into quasi-psychiatrists. The error of that tactic was proved by the case of social work, which as a profession so fell under the influence of psychiatry at one period of its history that the best-trained social workers retired to their offices to do psychotherapy, leaving a void in the community. There was then nobody left to do the kind of work for which this profession had been created; and it has taken social work many years to recover its identity and its basic mission. Consultants, therefore, try to ensure that while ministers incorporate greater psychological sophistication into their traditional religious role, they do not subordinate the values and techniques of their ministry to

newly discovered insights from another field. In the words of
one clergyman: "One of the things I learned from my consultant was the importance of doing what felt right to me as a
minister and as a man. So I did not try to adopt a different
style, but I learned to do my own thing more effectively."

Thus consultants do not persuade clergymen to "treat"
mental disturbances, although ministers may already cope
routinely and successfully with many forms of emotional illness, like depressions and obsessional neuroses among their parishioners. Rather, they try to help ministers differentiate between those conditions that are best treated by a mental
health specialist, and other cases, which may appear alarming
but which may be effectively dealt with by a competent clergyman. Without sufficient experience and support, a minister
might refer many of these latter conditions to psychiatric services, unnecessarily subjecting parishioners to waiting lists and
other obstacles to care, while helping to further clog access to
mental health facilities for more serious cases. He may also
help his parishioner to assume unnecessarily the expense, both
financial and emotional, of becoming a patient. On the other
hand, some clergymen mistake psychoses for milder conditions. They may try to manage them alone, and may thereby
inadvertently deprive a person of the medical treatment that
might cure him.

Consultation, unlike supervision and many other forms of
education, is designedly nonauthoritarian. The consultant and
consultee have coordinate status in their relationship with
each other. They are colleagues from different fields who have
come together to discuss a professional issue which is of importance to both. The consultee needs the consultant's help with a
current case that is overtaxing his capacity. The consultant
needs the consultee to succeed with that parishioner so that
the psychological well-being of the latter will be preserved or
improved; this in turn will advance the mental health of the
community. The consultant is not given any responsibility for
the client, nor any administrative power over the consultee,

who is free to accept or reject whatever the consultant says. Indeed, since the consultant is of another discipline, it is important that the consultee should be free to ignore suggestions
which would not fit his own professional culture and duties,
however valuable such prescriptions might have proved in a
clinical setting. Thus, although the consultant is superior to
the consultee in specialized knowledge about the psychosocial
aspects of the case, the consultee is superior to the consultant
in his knowledge of what is feasible and appropriate for a clergyman to do; and the consultee alone knows the parishioner
and has power to affect him. The consultant is not account-
able for the outcome of the parishioner's case, and therefore he
is not driven to impose his opinions on the minister.

Since the consultant has no power over the consultee, the
latter is never obliged to follow advice out of deference or fear.
He need accept only those suggestions that sound sensible and
that he believes will work. Paradoxically, this freedom to accept or reject ideas without the distracting complications of
hierarchical authority means that a consultee is in fact more
likely to experiment with a consultant's suggestions. That men
learn more readily without the emotional noise associated with
most educational relationships was observed by Dr. Samuel
Johnson in the eighteenth century, who held that for this reason the example of dead heroes and the written advice of
strangers was more palatable to most people than the same
counsel would be if it had come through direct contact:

We are not unwilling to believe that man wiser than ourselves, from
whose abilities we may receive advantage, without any danger of rivalry or opposition, and who affords us the light of his experience
without hurting our eyes by flashes of insolence. . . . An author cannot obtrude his advice unasked, nor can be often suspected of any
malignant intention to insult his readers with his knowledge or his
wit.

[*Rambler*, 87]

Consultation focuses exclusively on issues related to the formal work of consultees. A clergyman, in either an individual

or a group session, presents a current case which he finds particularly complicated; and that case, which may involve the counseling of a parishioner, an administrative problem within the church, or a question of community organization, remains the focus of discussion. As the case is dissected, the consultant concerns himself not primarily with the situation of the parishioner, the vestry, or the community, but rather, with identifying and improving those places where the clergyman is revealed as having difficulty in handling the situation.

As the minister describes the case, what emerges is not a picture of actual events, but rather, the clergyman's subjective view of those phenomena; he describes what he sees, not what a camera or a tape recorder would show. And what any person observes in a given situation is colored by his expectations, biases, and previous experiences with similar events, all of which may radically distort his view, making his responses inappropriate, and hence frustrating his attempts to help his parishioner.

As a consultant listens to the clergyman's description of a difficult case, therefore, he may find that certain parts of the story stand out by the way the consultee talks about them. There may be areas of exaggeration, confusion, or stereotyping in an otherwise coherent and balanced narrative. There may be inconsistencies within the story, as when a parishioner is described as standing alone in the world, when it is evident to a listener that in fact he has a normal complement of friends and relatives who are all concerned about him. The story may also reveal undue bias in favor of one of the characters involved and apparently unmerited antipathy to others. The minister may show great tension when he approaches certain points of the case history, or he may be inappropriately calm at others. If, for example, a clergyman spoke casually about a parishioner's threat of suicide, a consultant would prick up his ears.

Once these areas have been identified where the minister's

normal professional objectivity and judgment have been weakened, the consultant seeks possible reasons for the difficulty. The clergyman, for example, might be puzzled simply because the case requires more knowledge of psychosocial issues than he has yet mastered. His training might not have equipped him to cope with a particular problem of communication within complex systems, or an esoteric form of emotional abnormality, or it might not have taught him how to handle a population undergoing rapid change. A specialist consultant would supply such information as it is needed, allowing the minister to grasp a pattern in the hitherto inexplicable behavior of a parishioner or a community. At times, ministers have asked their consultants to give informal lectures on such topics as adolescent behavior, drug addiction, and current research on schizophrenia to keep their knowledge of theories in social science and psychiatry up to date.

Sometimes this lack of knowledge may make a clergyman unnecessarily anxious about a parishioner, since he assumes that the latter's symptoms are more ominous than, in fact, they are. Particular appreciation, therefore, was expressed by clergymen of an explanation offered in the course of a case consultation discussion about the types of, and expectable reactions to, the tranquilizers and stimulants which doctors commonly prescribe. Some men had been unduly alarmed when parishioners had come to them "on drugs," assuming that this attested to major disturbances. They were reassured when they learned about the actual properties of Librium and other mild sedatives, and the kind of cases where their use was indicated. In another consultation session, it became clear to the consultant that although many of these clergy had had years of experience in counseling alcoholics and their families, and knew the social and psychological causes and results of this condition, few understood the physiological effects of drinking. Thus there was considerable satisfaction when the consultant explained, again in connection with an actual case, what a "wet brain" was, when delirium tremens was likely to occur, and how alcohol dehydrates the body. It became clear that the ministers had always accepted these phenomena as mysteries which they had no hope of understanding or controlling. Once they heard brief explanations, however, they saw a logical pattern which could alter their own style of approaching such people. Since, for example, part of the mental deterioration of chronic alcoholics comes from organic damage caused by a vitamin deficiency, they wondered whether they could arrange with local physicians to supply vitamin capsules along with the coffee that all clergy seem to dispense to alcoholics who regularly arrive on their doorsteps.

Sometimes it appeared that a minister's puzzlement about psychological and medical factors in a parishioner's life was due not to gaps in his seminary training, or to few opportunities for continuing education after becoming ordained, but rather, to the difficulty in turning existing theoretical knowledge to full use in a concrete case. Consultation then provided a way in which a man's dormant knowledge could be made operational as it was shown to be applicable to a real-life situation.

When consultation becomes openly didactic, however, there is always a danger of muddying the boundary between clerical and mental health roles. One consultant explained: "I had to keep reminding myself not to treat the minister like a psychiatric resident. I wanted to tell him how to uncover more material and how to handle the next phase of transference. But I bit my tongue. I remembered that he had to handle the case in his own way."

Group consultation provides a safeguard here, because the ministers outnumber the consultant and can consequently protect their own style of professional functioning against suggestions which might fit psychiatric practice but do not suit the role of a clergyman. At one meeting, for example, the consultant psychiatrist suggested to a minister preoccupied with providing long-term care for an obviously hopeless chronic alcoholic—a man who, for years, had rotated in and out of every treatment facility in the area—that the clergyman disengage himself from the situation. "As a doctor," the consultant said, "I had to learn that I can't assume responsibility for such cases. Knowing they exist makes me feel miserable, it makes me feel terribly frustrated, but what can I do? I can't institutionalize people for the rest of their lives because they might get into trouble on their own. It's more humane to let them go their own way and run their own risks. Maybe you should just keep on making this man comfortable whenever he turns up, but you shouldn't worry so much about him freezing to death on a cold night when he camps out under a parked truck, or the fact that all the local hospitals tip him out as soon as they sober him up. You should differentiate *responsibility* from *concern.*"

The minister who had presented the case was so relieved by this lifting of his burden that he was not tempted to question the legitimacy of the consultant's suggestion. Other members of the group, however, who were not involved in the case and who could consequently react more objectively, protested this transfer of a medical model into their field. "But we *are* responsible for such people," a young clergyman insisted. "That is what we stand for as men of religion. We are *responsible,* not just concerned, for doing something about suffering in the community." The group then turned to exploring whether, indeed, the things clergy do for alcoholics and drug addicts, such as giving them handouts or even money to leave town, is an adequate expression of responsibility, or whether it is merely a way to shrug off the guilt that these people so skillfully inspire in those they approach for help. Other, potentially more productive, ways of treating them were suggested which would turn concern and responsibility into fruitful channels.

Sometimes ministers fumble with a case not because they lack understanding, but because they cannot find ways to ease the situation. Consultation can often help in sharpening skills; but, here also, there may be a danger to the integrity of a minister's role if he picks up mental health methodology, and a group of peers at a consultation session again provide the best safeguard. One man, for example, brought in an organizational problem. The population in his parish was changing from white to black, and, while supporting the newcomers, the minister suddenly found himself cut off from the original members of his congregation who were growing cold and hostile. How, he asked, was he to break through this blocked communication? One of his colleagues suggested that this segment of the case might be handled by delivering a sermon on a particular text which he supplied. The consultee thought this a useful idea and promised to try it. The consultant remarked later that while he had thought of a number of other ways for restoring contact, none was as simple and appropriate as that of a sermon.

Some men have difficulty counseling parishioners not because they lack knowledge or skill, but because they lack self-confidence. This is particularly true in cases where ministers suspect emotional disturbance in their parishioners, and where they fear that they might inadvertently damage a fragile personality. Consultation reassures clergymen by enabling them to submit the case to the inspection of colleagues and a clinician. The group will be likely to sense if the consultee is indeed mismanaging the situation, and will then suggest alternate ways of handling it; otherwise, they will validate his performance.

Some ministers lack self-confidence because, in helping parishioners with emotional problems, they rely not on a set of systemized procedures, but on intuition, wisdom, or trial and error. While a gifted clergyman may, in this way, achieve remarkable success in many cases, he may often be puzzled and even frightened by these very results, since he does not basically understand why his intervention worked. He may realize that without such knowledge he cannot rely on sustaining these results or on reproducing them, since the same techniques in an apparently similar case can inexplicably fail.

A college chaplain, for example, told of working with a depressed student who threatened suicide. For two sessions the student had set up a perpetual moan about what an intellectual, moral, and social fraud he was. At first the chaplain tried to reason with him, repeating, "Nonsense, you are very clever. You are clearly a decent person. You shouldn't tear yourself down like this." But he soon realized that he was only making the student more adamant. Suddenly, at the third session, when the case seemed more blocked than ever, the chaplain gave in to his intuition, and sarcastically mimicked the boy's own words, "Yes, you are right—you are rotten, lazy, and weak. People like you don't deserve to live!" The student was first stunned, and then began to defend himself hotly; and as he came to acknowledge another side of his character, the clergyman helped him to see that he might have a future after all.

The student left in a happier mood, but the minister was worried, even though he knew that there was a psychiatrist on the case. He had acted instinctively, not out of an understanding of the "anatomy of melancholy." Thus he did not know that he had stumbled onto one orthodox psychiatric technique for jerking people out of suicidal moods, and that the student was probably safe for the time being. He also did not know when to try his discovery again, since he was sophisticated enough to realize that if so drastic a method were used indiscriminately, it might prove catastrophic for some individuals. He even wondered whether this case were merely a fluke. "You can't tell in advance what will work," he insisted. "You have to feel around in each case and try different things. There don't seem to be any rules."

This chaplain, like many other ministers, was in a sense a gifted amateur. While an amateur may have flashes of brilliance and originality that surpass the work of a professional, his talent is unpredictable and his level of performance is likely to be uneven. A professional, on the other hand, may be pedestrian, but his work is more consistent, since he uses a self-conscious methodology which allows him to repeat his performance and to incorporate new techniques into a systematic framework and then to apply them to other cases. The amateur who wants to professionalize his work is like a musician who was a child prodigy. At some point, the little genius reaches the limit of what he can play by innate ability alone, and he must then return to drilling the dull fundamentals, with which he had never bothered before, but which he must master if he is to advance to higher levels of disciplined expression. The chaplain, lacking such a systematic basis for action, was unable to build up a repertory of tested skills, and so was forced to rely on the caprice of his own sensitivity and intuition in almost every case. This sapped his self-confidence, since he could never be certain that what worked once would ever work again; nor could he gain security from one success to feel that he might, in consequence, be more likely to avert another tragedy when the next suicidal student crept into his office.

One of the ways in which consultation can increase the self-confidence and precision of ministers is by helping them to assess why a particular technique worked, so that it can be confidently used again when it is indicated in another case. In this way, the minister's approach to disturbed people can be professionalized, but it will not become stereotyped, since an understanding of underlying principles can free clergy to make deliberate and precise innovations, rather than haphazard and fortuitous ones.

A painful source of difficulty which even well-trained, veteran clergymen may meet from time to time is not a lack of knowledge, skill, or self-confidence, but a loss of professional objectivity. In this they resemble all other categories of professionals; and it was to cope with this issue that the mental health consultation method described in this book was primarily developed and where it has been proved most helpful. When objectivity is lost, effective functioning is reduced. The professional distance which normally allows a minister to observe and counsel in other people's predicaments without sinking into their pain or their alliances and enmities suddenly deserts him. On some level, usually preconscious or unconscious, the clergyman now finds himself personally drawn into the action. Not only is this painful for him, but it is bad for his parishioners, since the minister's ability to offer sound help is constricted. This produces growing confusion and frustration as the situation refuses to be solved; and it often ends in lowered self-esteem when the minister feels that he has made a mess of the case and has become a fool in his own eyes.

A major aim of mental health consultation is to reduce those areas in which clergy are hindered in their efforts to help parishioners or to act in complex institutional and community problems because of such a loss of professional poise. It seeks to help a clergyman so handicapped to disentangle himself from sympathetic overidentification with the case, to restore his objectivity, to foster his *empathy* with the situation of all the people involved, and to enable him to *realistically* and rationally evaluate and cope with the problem, however emotionally taxing it might be. Further than that, it tries to help a minister so to overcome this lapse in professional functioning that in future cases of a similar kind he will not be as likely to get into the same difficulties again. Thus it is hoped that the consultee will be able to generalize from what he learns, so that his whole practice will benefit from the lessons of complex individual cases.

One might logically assume that, since the loss of professional objectivity is often triggered by preconscious or unconscious impulses, the best way to restore effective functioning would be by laying bare the minister's personal involvement in the case. It might be pointed out to him that his perception, for example, of a downtrodden husband succumbing to a domineering wife in a particular case is a distortion of the evidence; and that his taking sides in the situation shows that there must be a link with unresolved conflicts in his own personality. One might then perhaps help the minister to discover and solve his intra-psychic fears of "castration" by a powerful female. This would free him to manage with no further difficulties this and all future cases where apparently "weak" men are dominated by "bitchy" women.

Mental health consultation, however, deliberately avoids this course of action for a number of reasons. First, it is felt that to place normal functioning professionals into the dependent role of psychiatric patients, and to intrude on their private lives, often against their will, just because they are having difficulty with a case at work, is indecorous and unsound. If a professional's problems with his caseload were to be dealt with by uncovering unconscious conflicts, the consultant and the consultee would spend far too much time at this exercise, and would have little time left to serve their clients. Moreover, it is not clear that psychotherapy, especially in this informal framework, would really improve job performance anyway. Everyone has areas of irrationality in his personality, but most of us manage our affairs effectively despite them; and even disturbed people are able to perform remarkably well. There are some quite mad psychiatrists, for example, who are excellent therapists just because their own pathology allows them to understand and communicate with their patients. There does not seem to be a clear correlation, therefore, between "sanity" and doing a good job; so engaging in this kind of random uncovering might be both unpleasant for the professional and uneconomic for the community, since there would be no guarantee that once the time and money had been spent, the improvement would be significant.

Second, this uncovering of intra-psychic material might be dangerous. It is easy to reveal unconscious conflicts and fantasies, but only a suitably trained and disciplined expert will know how to manage the material once it emerges so that the patient will not be damaged by the experience. It is unfortunately a matter of record that some systems which attempt to teach people to handle interpersonal problems by conducting intra-psychic exploration, often in groups, have precipitated psychotic breakdowns in some of their clients. Not only are the personnel conducting these sessions often insufficiently trained, but it is difficult to keep perceptive members of the group from blurting out a possibly devastating interpretation.

Consultation, therefore, takes a safer, more economical route, and one that is more dignified for the consultee. Instead of stripping away the defenses of the personality in order to dig out unconscious material, consultation tries to strengthen these defenses, shore up the ego at its weaker points, and enable the individual to function better and more comfortably, even though he, like most of humanity, might never be a paragon of mental health and maturity. A consultant, therefore, sets out to help a clergyman, as a fellow worker carrying out a professional job, to master his emotional difficulties with a case, and to accomplish this without tampering with the man's private life, since that is nobody's business but his own.

Nevertheless, the effectiveness of consultation depends, paradoxically, precisely on the consultant's recognition and identification, *though never his explicit mention,* of the emotional entanglement of the minister with his case. For this is often a key to the clergyman's perplexity; and it is by using this understanding that the man's objectivity can most readily be restored.

A clergyman, for example, might have problems in handling a case if he were to become emotionally involved with one or more of the people he is trying to help. Instead of relating to such individuals through his professional role, as a minister with a parishioner, he relates to them personally. It is interesting, for instance, that some clergy bring up cases in which they have been having difficulty advising old friends, or, in one rather dramatic instance, an old enemy. In the latter case, a minister had been appealed to by a vestryman desperate over a rebellious son, and it became clear that the minister was fighting to keep himself from attacking the man who had made his own life a misery for months over the church budget, and who was now enticingly vulnerable.

In this kind of situation, the consultant and a group of peers become models for the consultee of how to reestablish correct professional distance. By the way they question and comment about the material in the case, they help the presenter to achieve professional empathy instead of undue involvement with, or distance from, the person he is duty-bound to help. This can be managed without any loss of face for the consultee, because his involvement is never explicitly labeled and condemned. Nobody, for instance, suggested to the clergyman mentioned earlier that the source of his difficulty in helping the vestryman lay in his own barely conscious satisfaction that this parishioner was getting his just deserts. Had they confronted him with this, a conscientious and humane minister would have been made to feel ashamed and guilty for harboring malice. Instead of forcing him to look at his uncharitable feelings, therefore, the group nudged the consultee with questions and speculations about the facts of the case into looking at his parishioner's situation from a more objective angle, where the man's human needs began to take precedence over his tightfistedness at vestry meetings.

Another common reason for losing professional objectivity is *overidentification*, when the minister takes sides. Usually this is easy to recognize because the clergyman will speak of one character with uncritical approval, while other figures are spoken of with animosity, often with little evidence put forward to support this disapproval. Sometimes, the reason for this overidentification is relatively clear, since the conditions of the minister and the parishioner may be superficially similar. They may both be near retirement age; they may both have nagging wives, or slipped discs, or a taste for modern art. Or the source of the kinship may lie only in the recesses of the minister's unconscious mind. Whatever the similarity, the clergyman fails to take into account the actual merits of the case, and instead makes up his mind about it because of his own personal associations with a similar, but far from identical, situation.

The *reason* for the overidentification is not important; the *fact* of it is. Whatever the reason may be, the consultant must get the minister to look at the case again, in a new and more realistic light, and to see around the stereotypes which he has created. The consultant, by the way he talks about the parishioner or vestryman, or curate, can help the consultee to realize that this person may not, in fact, be quite as he first thought he was, and that even if the bad people are just as poisonous as the minister feared, a professional can empathize even with their condition and can help ease their discomfort, too.

A clergyman recounted a complex case of marital infidelity, for example, in which he was clearly identifying with the husband but was counseling the wife. He was convinced that he would never be able to help the injured woman, whom he described as middle-aged, unattractive, domineering, and deaf. "If I were married to her," he said, "I'd play around, too!" He mentioned in passing that part of his difficulty in helping her came from the sheer burden of trying to communicate, a problem which he felt the husband shared. The consultant asked if the woman wore a hearing aid. The clergyman said that she did not. The consultant asked why that was. The clergyman said firmly that hearing aids were useful only in certain cases, but not in nerve deafness—there was nothing that could be done for such people. The consultant persisted. Had the woman sought treatment for her deafness? Was she indeed nerve deaf? It gradually emerged that the clergyman had never asked her; instead he had jumped to a number of conclusions. Since she was not wearing a hearing aid, she must be nerve deaf because he had heard that there was no way to help nerve-deaf people. So her case was hopeless, just as he had known from the beginning, since she was so unattractive and domineering that her husband could not help but leave her, and she would inevitably be crushed by his desertion. The consultant pointed out that deafness is often used to shut out an unacceptable world. He began to talk with sympathetic understanding about the woman's predicament. Suddenly, the clergyman remembered that this woman used her handicap in order to manipulate conversations, selectively ignoring advice and carrying on monologues of recrimination against her husband. He wondered whether he might break through this barrier if he were sufficiently firm, and whether he might urge her to seek medical advice. Gradually, he began to realize that this unpleasant stereotype was a complicated human being who might be communicated with and helped after all.

A third, but related, cause for losing professional objectivity is *transference*, when a minister reads into a parishioner's case aspects of his own life, imposing a pattern on the client's situation taken from his own condition. This produces the "bees-in-the-bonnet phenomenon" when a particular clergyman can always be counted on to mishandle a certain type of situation. Somehow, for example, a higher-than-average proportion of his marital-counseling cases end in divorce; or he always gets involved in fights with the congregation over curates who make inflammatory sermons—other rectors find nice curates, but this one is always landed with a fanatic; or every time he has to officiate at a deathbed, he panics and retreats into aloofness and cold, formulaic responses to hide his misery. Here, once again, the objectivity of a sympathetic outsider can help a consultee find new perspectives on cases that have always seemed impossible to him, and which are made more so every time a new one comes along to rank as another failure on the minister's record.

In another of these categories where professional objectivity is lost, a minister displaces an unresolved, personal emotional problem onto one of his cases. He unconsciously avoids facing his own problem, and instead becomes preoccupied with a similar dilemma in the life of the parishioner. This allows him to grapple with the issue that is pressing on him, but without the extra tension and loss of self-esteem that would be involved if he had to confront the problem in his own life and admit his own personal failure. But since it was often an irrational expectation of such failure that had always prevented him from dealing directly with the issue and mastering it in his own life, this also influences the way he handles the problem in his parishioner. He becomes convinced, often in the teeth of the evidence, that the case must end badly.

This conviction of poor outcome is apt to constrict his view of the situation and to cause him to jump to stereotyped conclusions. His subjective involvement prevents him from collecting and weighing the evidence with his customary care and skill, and he is likely to repeat a few ineffectual methods of intervention rather than to plan a course of constructive action that is tailored to the feasible possibilities of the actual situation. Indeed, the clergyman's automatic reactions, based upon his constricted perceptions of the case, often load the dice against his parishioner and validate the clergyman's irrational expectations of failure. This usually leads to an impasse. The clergyman finds himself preoccupied with his parishioner's problem, but with a mounting sense of frustration and professional failure and with the feeling of being trapped in a situation out of which there is no productive path, only the one or two ways that he has already repeatedly tried and found wanting.

Consultants recognize this type of predicament when a clergyman talks with great emotional intensity about certain aspects of a parishioner's problem that seem to have some special significance to him, though they seem less critical to an outsider, and then jumps to stereotyped judgments about a poor outcome that are not rationally based on the evidence. In many such situations, the clergyman seems to be looking at the parishioner and his family with tunnel vision that permits him to see only what he expects to find, a pathway to disaster. Then the minister compulsively struggles to stave off what he foresees to be inevitable. But whatever he does only serves to hasten failure; and he does not seem able to realize that there would be alternate possibilities both for the parishioner and for the efficacy of his own intervention if he could only expand his view of the situation to take more factors into account.

A minister, for example, told his consultant about a middle-aged parishioner who had been trying for some weeks to decide whether to leave his wife and family, or whether to give up his attachment to a girl whom he did not love but whom he found pathetically vulnerable and therefore fascinating. Although the parishioner was an unaggressive man, in the course of an argument with his wife about their situation, he slapped her face. When he told the clergyman of this, the latter had responded, "According to my experience, you must be on the verge of a nervous breakdown."

Nothing that the minister subsequently described to the consultant warranted that assumption; but for the consultee, the case formed a pattern which could lead to only one outcome. The parishioner was delaying a complicated emotional decision, and was consequently under strain. When he then gave way to an aggressive urge, the minister could interpret this in only one way: the parishioner was losing all self-control, and this was the sign of the onset of a nervous breakdown.

An objective outsider could have seen that the man's outburst was probably an isolated incident, which, in fact, reduced his tension. Moreover, according to the minister's own narrative, the parishioner was working at his own feelings and trying to assess what course of action would do the least harm. But the clergyman's view was fixed; he could not conceive of anything that could avert catastrophe for a man who lost control of aggression after undergoing protracted strain.

The consultant first searched for the point where the minister's perception of the case constricted his expectation, where he was reacting automatically instead of continuing to consider the evidence. Once the consultant found that spot, he did not try to explore reasons in the minister's private life that accounted for this sensitivity. Instead, he supported the clergyman in examining this upsetting case afresh to see if indeed it was hopeless, or if, as was far more likely, they could not together find a fresh perspective that would broaden the consultee's view of the range of alternatives to which his parishioner's actions might lead.

Instead of concluding that there could be only one end for a man under strain who lost control over hostile impulses, the minister came to realize that the evidence pointed to alternative possibilities. The man might indeed have a nervous breakdown; but he might also be sobered by his outburst, and might therefore resolve to control himself more vigilantly until his difficult decision was made. The clergyman could now return to his parishioner not only with a more optimistic and complicated understanding of the case and with an increased range of options where his own efforts could be effective, but also freed from unrealistic and distracting preoccupations. Instead of spending all his time worrying about averting a nervous breakdown that was in fact unlikely to occur, the minister would be free to concentrate on helping the man to solve his actual and pressing problem.

Once the consultee's objectivity has returned, once he has been able to double back and rethink a hitherto automatic response, he will be more likely to face similar cases more judiciously in the future, since he will have realized that the cues which have always had only one fatal meaning for him do not necessarily lead to failure. This will help his parishioners; it will also have a therapeutic effect on the consultee. Since his difficulties with the case were based on the fact that it was a displacement object for the same problem in himself, finding that there was a chance of a good outcome for the parishioner might suggest that he himself could be equally fortunate. Thus, that clergyman would be less likely to fear for his own stability when, for example, while under strain, he himself was tempted to give way to anger.

This form of intervention can succeed only if it is conducted in a friendly, supportive atmosphere. It will fail utterly if a consultant or members of a consultation group attempt to joke or shame a minister out of his fears, or if they root around in his private life to show him why he is reacting irrationally. In order for a man to have the courage to reexamine evidence about an issue that he is convinced is hopeless and upsetting, and to accept fresh perspectives when he has long been trapped by one view, he must be able to rely on those to whom he has turned for help. Since he comes in a moment of weakness, he must be certain that nobody will attack him. It is the role of the consultant, particularly in group sessions, to create and maintain a companionable atmosphere where only tact and civility are allowed, and where the sensibilities of all the members of the group are respected.

The contrasting effects of civilized and hostile interventions were demonstrated in a group that was testing consultation for the first time. The members had known each other for some years and, as a group, had experimented with a number of ways to help participants with their problems. One man volunteered to present a case, and it was a mark of its urgency for him, as well as of his courage, that he was prepared to risk an unknown venture to find a way out of his dilemma.

In his parish, he said, the church organization had always run smoothly. Every year he would approach a few wealthy and efficient men and would ask them to serve on the vestry. A *pro forma* election was held; the congregation ratified the clergyman's choice; and the vestry thus formed obeyed the rector with little argument. This system, he said, had a number of advantages. It enabled him to retain control; it ensured that the work of the parish was done, since the man chosen to oversee the maintenance of the churchyard, for instance, was willing and able to do the job; and it kept wealthy parishioners in a mood to contribute to the church budget.

Last year, however, this tidy system had broken down. A new head warden, an "old goat," went over to the "liberals," and allowed fifteen nominations to be made for five vacancies on the vestry. The unheard of number of 550 people turned out for the election, and all five places went to liberal candidates. Now elections were scheduled again, and the clergyman feared that more power would go to these "upstarts."

The rector found the situation "terrifying." He said that he had looked out at all those faces assembled in the church hall for the election, and he had "hated it." He felt not only that he was losing personal control, but that this new system would tear the community apart. Vestry elections would become politicized; the active men who could be relied on to get a job done would be replaced by radicals who were only seizing the limelight and did not really care about the church; and, most painful, the "money men" might find the whole situation so offensive that they might withhold donations.

"I know," the minister continued, "that it's probably all my fault. If I could make up my mind to accept the new order, I guess we could get along somehow. I'm not even sure that I want to go back to the undemocratic way. But, as I see it, with this system everything can't help but go downhill."

In the ensuing discussion, mediated by the consultant, comments of the other clergymen fell into two categories. The first and largest was made up of suggestions which indeed sought to broaden the presenter's view of the probable outcome of the case, but which were also veiled attacks on the consultee. Some made fun of the man's authoritarian philosophy and said that they could not understand anyone who was not elated by 550 people coming to a church meeting. Others, quickly ruled out of order by the consultant, said that the problem was obviously in the rector's own mind; if he could take a saner view of the matter, he would realize that no catastrophe was likely to occur. The consultee said, "Yes, I know, I'm probably crazy. But, so what? I'm the rector and this is my vestry—how do I handle it?" Other members of the group told, rather smugly, of how well they had handled similar revolutions in their own parishes, and suggested that the presenter use the same techniques of hiring extra people to do the work of the parish, or finding fresh ways of soothing rich donors. Still others tried to prove that the liberals were unlikely to be a threat at all. They were, as the consultee himself admitted, established members of the community, not outside agitators; and while they might be a bit more paranoid than right-thinking conservatives, they might only want recognition, and might not be intent on dragging the church down after all.

Another member of the group, however, used a different tone. Perhaps, he suggested, the rector might circumvent the vestry. The new people could then take the prominent positions, but the minister could create subcommittees, manned by his own reliable men, to do the real work. In this way, even if the liberals succeeded in taking over, the parish would still function. Some time later, another colleague said that the example of one of his own neighbors might help the consultee. Five years ago, threatened with a similar revolution, this clergyman had created a nominating committee. The members were elected for a term of six months in order to study the qualifications of all potential candidates for the vestry. They took their job seriously, and were endowed with high prestige. They made sure that the people who appeared on the final slate were all suitable for the work and respected in the community. So far, the colleague continued, his neighbor's parish was managing nicely. "Those are the answers I was looking for!" said the consultee. "It's a third way, not the old, undemocratic system, and not this new mess. It's a way out, and it feels right."

What was particularly interesting here was that in the en-

suing discussion of why the consultation experiment had succeeded, the consultee said that he could clearly differentiate
between comments made in a helpful way and comments
which might have looked helpful on the surface, but which
were really covert attacks on his philosophy, his sanity, and his
intelligence. In trying to argue with, and shame him out of, an
illogical position, his colleagues only made him feel more be-
leaguered, thus driving him deeper into rigidity and defensive-
ness. He could not, without losing his dignity, accept any of
their suggestions even if one of them had offered a real alternative.

Those who had suggested creating subcommittees of the vestry and a nominating body, however, had reacted directly to
the consultee's need without judging him. And the consultee
could later describe the sense of companionship that was immediately created. He felt that these men's contributions were
focused directly on the issue that troubled him. They did not
quibble about whether the rector's discomfort was warranted
by objective reality; they accepted his definition of the problem and addressed themselves to that point. The rector, therefore, could accept their advice, first, he said, because it was on
target, and second, because in doing so, he made no admission
of bigotry, eccentricity, or stupidity, as he would have done
had he accepted the suggestions of some of the other members
of the group.

Another interesting point that emerged was that the consultee had no doubt that while gaining an intellectually
broader view of his options in this situation he had also received considerable emotional relief. His worry, frustration,
and sense of being trapped had been lifted. Even though the
consultant had not allowed any discussion of the roots of his
feelings, this transaction had not been a purely intellectual
process. Nor should this have surprised anyone. It is naïve in
the extreme to imagine that the only way to obtain emotionally significant results is to deal with feelings directly—to un-

dress, as it were, and get emotional about them. Such charged material can often be more effectively dealt with rationally, coolly, and with decorum.

Consultation, therefore, serves as a vehicle for education and support for handling difficult work situations. It helps ministers to gain greater sophistication about psychosocial issues; but it also attempts to increase objectivity and judgment by strengthening the boundaries that keep the problems of private life out of the professional's work. By training ministers in problem-solving techniques that stress the importance of exploring real evidence instead of jumping to conclusions, it helps consultees reduce distortions in perception that are triggered by aspects of their own lives. It can also help professionals to deal with some of their own unsolved personal problems, not by exposing them, but by helping them to manage successfully cases among their parishioners that have reflexive meaning for themselves.

chapter 4

Lessons of an Unsuccessful Case

It is often easier to abstract the principles of a technique while it is applied unsuccessfully than to understand its working during a polished performance when it flows smoothly and effortlessly. Let us examine the following case, therefore, in which not only was the presenter hampered by subjective involvement in his parishioners' situation, but other clergy in the group and *the consultant* lost their objectivity, too. Nevertheless, even within the confusion, and despite a host of technical errors which the consultant allowed himself to fall into, the clergyman seeking help did get some support and reassurance, and some general increase in understanding was achieved for the group.

The case was presented by Mr. Waters, a minister in his late fifties, who had always given evidence of sophistication about psychological issues. Because of his competent manner and warm personality, the consultant had special respect for him, and came to regard him as a resource to whom questions about the "proper" functions of a minister in any awkward situation could be referred.

Waters had been troubled recently, he said, by the plight of retired men unable to cope with leisure. "As people approach retirement," he continued, "you get a completely different perspective on time. The only good time is when you are busy or active, and people grow very fearful of time on one's hands. These people don't seem to appreciate this honest freedom. I want to share this problem with you, which I think will grow more prevalent as we go along."

The wives of such men, Waters went on, complain that their husbands are forever underfoot, growing dependent on them for suggestions of things to do.

"In our preachments, our own attitudes, our verbalizations, we say one ought to look forward to retirement. This is something that can be rewarding. And yet, when we come to the facing of it, we find that there is a fear that develops in the sphere of reaching this particular age, also the attitude on how to utilize time."

The consultant noted the shifting pronouns, the awkward syntax uncharacteristic of the man, and the fact that Waters and two other members of the group were nearing retirement age themselves; and he realized that this topic was likely to evoke emotionally charged material close to the surface of individual and group consciousness. In order, therefore, to prevent the consultee and the other clergy from openly identifying with, and being threatened by, discussion of the various problems to which Waters had just alluded—aging, retirement, use of leisure, dependency, etc.—the consultant firmly and wisely declined to deal with this subject in the abstract, and suggested that more fruitful results would emerge if they examined an actual case. In this way, he hoped to keep potentially painful ideas impersonal and distant enough so that those who might be sensitive to them could look at them "out there," with a measure of professional detachment, instead of facing them as they directly affected their own private lives.

The consultant had experienced the dangers of another course of action when, at some earlier sessions, he had allowed discussion to proceed in general terms about such delicate subjects as the extent of the rector's control over the financial affairs of his parish, or how clergy might best minister to the dying. These sessions proved singularly unrewarding. Discussion was either so abstract as to bore the participants, one man saying, "This generalizing about what to do with dying people is a waste of time. We deal with individuals, not categories. These ideas are useful only when they are pegged to a case"; or they allowed these sensitive issues to float ominously over the company, with no displacement object to buffer them, until inevitably someone was struck by their application to himself and, warmed by the intimate atmosphere of the group, he then proceeded to pour out his personal feelings. One minister, now revealed for the first time as engaged in a bitter feud with his vestry, passionately and embarrassingly denounced his community's power to curb his programs and take his job. At another session, a man who had sat in silence for over an hour, suddenly said in a shaken voice that he felt dazed by this discussion of techniques to help the dying, since he was traumatized each time he was called to carry out that part of his role and he would rather not think about it more than he could help. It was noticeable that after each such session, the number of participants in the group dropped, as though clergy were wary of exposing themselves to sudden confrontations with emotionally laden material when their defenses were lowered.

So in this case, the consultant was wise to suggest that, rather than discussing retirement in the abstract, the group would be better served if Waters could describe an actual case. The consultee readily agreed, launching at once into a current counseling problem which, in resisting his efforts, had clearly motivated the general and pregnant question with which he had already opened his presentation.

The case concerned a retired man and his resourceful, competent wife. The husband had been an executive in a brokerage firm and had retired a year ago; the wife still worked, writing short stories for women's magazines and performing occasionally in the local community theater. At first, after his retirement, the husband had found little to do, and had "come to the point" of doing a "menial task," of selling magazine subscriptions over the phone for a few hours every morning. In the afternoons, he would return home "with the sense of 'What will I do now?' " His wife had recently come to Waters in despair, since the magazine had stopped its telephone subscription service, and her husband was now idle all day. He was willing to do anything, but he expected his wife to take all the initiative. He was "all thumbs around the house," so he was no help with the chores; and his wife now feared that she had "another child on her hands."

"Did you know the man before?" the consultant asked. "Are you surprised by this reaction to retirement, or would you have predicted this lack of initiative?"

Waters seemed puzzled by the question and answered tentatively, "He has initiative, but no self-confidence." The man, it appeared, had shown no enthusiasm for finding a new job, although Waters had suggested several types of voluntary work. He was not much interested, the minister continued, in the company of men, although he had worked with them all his life. Waters had tried, again unsuccessfully, to prod him into joining a retired men's club, where his fine singing voice and skill in public speaking would have been an asset to the group. But the man did not feel the problem as his wife did, and showed no inclination to do more with his time. She, on the other hand, "feels literally hemmed in," complaining to the minister that her husband does not realize that he is so demanding. Furthermore, whenever she pointed out her discomfort to her husband, he grew hurt and depressed, "almost as though she had spanked him."

Already a pattern was emerging in Waters's presentation. The husband was described negatively on the whole, as inexplicably idle, childish, and emasculated. There were significant patches of vagueness in the narrative, as when the minister was unable to describe the parishioner's character before retirement. It was as though Waters saw the man's present state as bearing no connection to the rest of his life, or as though he had never given the man much thought as a person before, and was now considering him for the first time. In either case, this overlooking of the parishioner's past was significant. Further, the words with which he was described were somewhat exaggerated: he took a "menial job," he acted, when remonstrated with, as though his wife had "spanked him." On the other hand, the wife was described approvingly. The evidence for a loss of professional objectivity on Waters's part, therefore, was strong.

Now the consultant should have begun to explore the material closely to learn where the minister's main concern lay— where his view of the situation seemed to be constricted. He should have traced, for example, Waters's sources of information. In whose judgment was the man idle, dependent, and at a loss for things to do? Was this the view of the husband, the wife, or Waters? Instead of continuing to examine the material systematically, however, the psychiatrist launched into a hasty explanation of the case. "This woman's frustration," he said firmly, "doesn't surprise me at all." Followed by other members of the group, he then gave examples of how difficult it is when men break into a woman's routine by staying home during the day. He even described the domestic crisis that was caused when he himself had been confined to the house for four days with flu until his wife "nearly went mad." How much worse it is, the group agreed, when the man is retired, and the woman must adjust to never having the house to herself. One minister commented that the career pattern of a housewife runs opposite to that of her husband. As a woman gets older and her children leave, she finds herself less tied to the house and more involved in community affairs; but retirement brings the man back into the home. Thus a woman is apt to find her newly won freedom snatched away.

The group was now engaged in the fruitless exercise of making judgments about the case before the evidence was gathered. In doing so, they had little hope of relieving Waters's concern, since they had not listened long enough to find out what that concern might be. The group and the consultant were not only wasting time, but were also practicing a pattern of problem-solving which consultation ideally tries to discourage, a pattern in which one jumps to the conclusion, triggered by scanty evidence, that a case fits into a certain category. That categorization then determines the professional's future treatment of, and expectations for, the case. Here, therefore, the consultant and the group were reinforcing each other and Waters in a bad habit.

Furthermore, premature interventions of this kind can be hazardous. At this stage of the presentation, one may readily identify areas of sensitivity in the consultee, but one has as yet no way of knowing what the heightened language, the tense manner, and the other signs of concern may mean. Unless restraint is used, therefore, one is apt to find that one has pushed matters in just the wrong direction, raising the consultee's level of concern rather than diminishing it.

In this case, the consultant and the group quickly realized that in Waters's eyes the parishioner's passivity and aimlessness and the wife's irritation at his constant company were of central concern. The consultee presented it as the main feature of the case, and he did so in an emotionally weighted manner. But what was it in the nature of this situation that he found so aggravating? Was it the discontent of the wife, whom the minister clearly admired? Was it her rejection of her husband's needs after years of marriage? Was it the retired man's loss of adult initiative and his reversion to childish dependency? Or was it a far more subtle cue that pressed on Waters at an unconscious level which set this case apart from all other superficially similar ones, and which impelled the consultee to seek the group's help with *this* case, rather than with that of another retired couple or another husband who was overly dependent on his wife? Unless consultant and group listen patiently to a consultee's exposition, suspending judgment until they have questioned him at length on the details of his parishioner's dilemma, they will be unlikely to isolate the node of his difficulty; and the force of the entire consultation will then be largely blunted.

In this instance, far from enlightening Waters with their comments, the consultant and the group unwittingly strengthened one of his exaggerated concerns arising from the case—that women are indeed trapped and driven to desperation by men who, by the loss of their proper role through retirement, are made unmanly dependents of their wives. Moreover, the manner of the intervention was subtly belittling. It implied that the situation that the consultee had been agonizing over for days or weeks was in fact so transparent that others could resolve it after a ten-minute hearing. This could be a particularly tactless thing to imply to a man who might be raising the case out of desperation, having come to doubt his own abilities on this occasion, and whose self-respect might thus be vulnerable.

There were, however, two minor, positive elements in this episode which should not be overlooked. First, it developed active participation by most members of the group at an early stage of the session, rather than leaving the consultee in sole possession of the floor. Second, it humanized the consultant. Instead of assuming the stereotyped psychiatric pose of impersonality, distance, and nonreaction, he showed himself by the anecdote of his own attack of flu to be a man among men, a person who could share a serio-comic experience with his friends and equals.

Many clergy have spoken appreciatively of consultants who could set aside their clinical pose to become in this way real members of the group. They also told of their discomfort with other psychiatrists who were unable to shed the aloof manner

into which they had been drilled. These men, although nomi-
nally coordinate with their consultees, seemed to cling to the
vestiges of the hierarchical doctor-patient relationship while
they listened to the group sharing stories of their children and
grandchildren, but never offered similar confidences themselves. One minister said: "We wondered about our consultant
for months. He never revealed anything about himself and
seemed to brush aside any overtures and attempts to develop a
personal relationship. He seemed to want so much to stay objective and clinical. But we were all colleagues, we called each
other by our first names, and it was sort of peculiar having this
fellow there who remained a consultant to the group, instead
of a member of the group, if you see what I mean. Then
finally, we got one of the fellows to ask him if he was married
and if he had any kids. We wanted to know if his knowledge
about relationships was real, or only theoretical."

In the discussion of Waters' case, however, the consultant
was already known to the group as a warm and friendly person with whom they all felt at ease, so from the point of view of
building and maintaining a relationship, this personal anecdote was really a superfluous interruption: an interruption,
moreover, which subtly linked the topic back to "my experiences," how "my wife and I felt when we got in each other's
way in the kitchen," rather than stressing that the focus was
out there, on Waters' case.

Meanwhile, Waters listened patiently while the group wan-
dered off on its fishing expedition, and he gradually edged his
way back into the discussion. He agreed that his retired parishioner tied his wife down, but he insisted that this was a
more complex problem than the familiar picture that his colleagues were creating of a woman who had married "for better
or for worse, but not for lunch." The problem lay, he insisted,
in the man's inexplicable behavior. Even when he had been
leaving for his part-time job in the morning, he had expected
to find his wife waiting at home when he returned in the mid-

dle of the day. If she was out, he was hurt. And although he would gladly accompany her to the rehearsals of plays in which she appeared, he would not move about alone. "He's with her all the time, and she doesn't feel it's wholesome."

"How," asked the consultant, "does the man regard his own retirement? Is it any kind of problem?"

"He's loving it!" snapped Waters. "And that's the awkwardness of the whole situation. He enjoys reading spy stories and sleeping late. He is growing more and more passive and dependent and losing all the interests he used to have."

The consultant asked how the man felt about his wife's state of upset. The minister said that she, unlike other wives, adjusted to the situation on the surface, although she worried underneath, afraid that as her husband clung closer to her, he would usurp more and more of her time. She had urged him to act alone, but, she said, this always precipitated "this hurt feeling," and she no longer dared to work energetically to change the situation.

More elements in the pattern of the case were here emerging. There was obviously a blockage of communication between the husband and wife—although Waters did not seem to formulate it in those terms, since his bias in favor of the wife led him to ascribe the problem exclusively to the wrong-headedness of the husband.

"Has the wife noticed any changes over the year of her husband's retirement?" the consultant asked.

"Yes," said Waters. "There's less initiative to reach out, and more of what I call 'usurping' of her time."

"How old are they," asked Mr. Moss, another clergyman, "sixty-fivish?"

"No, he's seventy-one and she's sixty-two."

"That's quite a difference in age," remarked a curate.

"Wasn't it rather a change for the man to sell subscriptions after being an executive?" Mr. Green asked.

"Oh, he gives the impression of not caring about it. He's

perfectly happy with his noninvolvement."

"Do they try to travel a bit? Many retired people do."

"No. They have a limited income, only a pension; and their two married children live in this area. They are a closely knit family and visit back and forth, but the man doesn't take much joy in his grandchildren, and can tolerate them for only a short period. The man has no interests and no honest abilities around the house."

"Does the man have a different idea of himself since retirement?" the consultant asked. "Is he showing other signs of change than just having more spare time?"

"He's not senile," Waters answered. "He's not lazy either. To a degree, he has always leaned on his wife; she's always been the resourceful one. But his work gave him prestige."

The curate again said that he was struck by the great difference in the ages of the husband and wife. A woman in her early sixties might have certain expectations of her husband which a man in his early seventies might not be able to meet. "I think," he said, "that someone who is seventy-one is . . . , well is . . ." He was drowned out by nervous laughter from the older men in the room. "Someone of sixty-one may be very young," he continued loudly. "And I know people in their seventies and eighties who are full of vitality; but that's more rare. It's harder for most people to be still expanding their vision at that age."

The issue of age was clearly significant. It was unusual for Waters not to have mentioned the disparate ages of his parishioners when he first described them—most consultees give such vital statistics at once. Moreover, when the curate raised the subject twice, it was twice dropped after nervous laughter; so while the young man might have been very perceptive in suggesting that it was a factor in the actual case, it might also have indicated the consultee's further lack of objectivity in failing to take account of it, and also the group's sensitivity in deliberately refusing to pursue it in discussion. This was the first sign of the other ministers' growing embroilment in, and consequent difficulty with, the case.

"Can't they work as a team around the house?" asked Mr. White.

"No," said Waters. "He's completely incompetent. And she's frustrated, because if she tries to talk to him about it, there's that hurt. And he just hangs about, with no hope of being an influence on town politics or anything else."

Waters was here signaling that the discussion was off course, and he was consequently restating the issues that bothered him. This tenacity is characteristic of consultation: if interventions are inappropriate, the consultee's level of concern is such that he will unconsciously reiterate his problem until someone hears him. If nobody strikes to the core of his dilemma in one case, he will be likely to return with the story of another parishioner in which he has encountered identical underlying issues, in the unconscious hope that this time he will learn the solution. In this present case, tension mounted as Waters, unsatisfied by peripheral contributions, refused to be deflected from what were for him the salient issues. As he restated his main concerns over and over again, the group became strangely fascinated by the repetition, and were significantly swayed by it, as we will see.

"Is it that your parishioner has no hope of influencing things, or no interest?" the consultant asked.

"Well, that's the funny thing. When you look at him you'd think he was the most happy guy. He probably wasn't that concerned about things when he was working either. She was always the person with depth, with the stronger personality, pushing him."

"The only case of retirement I know really well," Mr. Apple said, "was my uncle, and I think these cases must be similar. I remember that when he had been retired for a while, anyone else might have had a nervous breakdown. In those days, of course, you didn't have such things, you just sweated it out.

My uncle got very tense and couldn't sleep till he finally went to the doctor. The doctor saw what was wrong and called my cousins, their children, into this, because, although my aunt and uncle had planned very well for retirement, the one thing they had never considered or discussed was the need for independence; they didn't think that loving, well-bred people should need it. So my uncle's problem was eased when one of his sons suggested that he soundproof his den so that he wouldn't hear the television or my aunt's bridge club, which had been driving him crazy. He also had a greenhouse built at the end of the garden so he could have a life apart from the household. This was best done with more than two people discussing it. The children legitimized the fact that when a man gives up his responsibilities he has a new life, and the wife's life, in a way, continues independent of his."

"But what I hear," said the consultant, "is that while the wife in Joe Waters's case says she wants her husband to be independent, what she really wants is to get him out of her hair, and she doesn't really care what he does, as long as he is out of her way."

This was not a wise remark. First, it ignored Apple's story, which had opened the subject of how to deal with blocked communication in such a case. Apple had listened carefully, and had heard Waters allude to this issue three or four times already. He realized its centrality both to the husband and wife and to the minister, who was clearly at a loss over how to restore understanding between the spouses. The consultant not only failed to pick this up, but he took off in another direction that was unwise for two reasons: first, it made a statement about the case, instead of asking questions about the material in order to stimulate Waters to reexamine it; and second, it had a blaming, unprofessional tone. Waters had already shown that he blamed the husband and sympathized with the wife. The consultant was not modeling a professional attitude when he, in turn, condemned the woman.

"No," Waters said, "it's odd you should have this impression. What bothers her is that they can't approach this in discussion so that he can appreciate that he's around *all the time.* He thinks this is just wonderful, and he can't see that she wants an opportunity to do a few things without the sense that she must be home before him, otherwise he'll be hurt."

"How does she present this to him when he seems to get depressed?" An excellent question, since it was working around to isolating the communication problem. Waters, however, did not face it.

"He does get depressed—that's the nature of the guy," he answered.

"Are we figuring that it's upsetting for him to come back to an empty house?" the consultant asked.

"That's right."

"We're figuring that's quite hard on him?"

"That's right."

"How hard is 'hard'?"

A long pause. The consultant was now trying to reduce to rational bounds Waters' possibly exaggerated concern that the husband would be devastated by his wife's absence, based on measured experience, rather than on fantasy and heightened language.

"Suppose she said, 'I'll be back by four'; would that satisfy him?"

"With the children, she could do this, but not with this guy. He expects that she be there, and he doesn't appreciate the fact that it's a change for her to be tied like this. And yet, he isn't dictatorial, he isn't a hard person."

"So he depends on his wife's initiative; and when she takes initiative for herself, and acts on her own, he is hurt because he isn't included," the consultant summarized. "He wants to be mothered, and she isn't eager to have another kid."

"That's it," said Waters grimly.

"The question is," the consultant continued, "how many of

her suggestions to him come from her considering what is best for him, and how many about what's best for her?" The consultant was now hovering near the target. "By now, he can probably pick up that there is some self-interest on her part, and each suggestion is a possible rejection. He might not take any suggestions from her because he's getting suspicious of what they mean."

"This has gotten to be a real hang-up for her," Waters said.

"That must make any suggestions coming from her very sticky," the consultant continued.

"Well," the minister said, "they go over his head very neatly."

"He doesn't want to hear them," said Moss.

"They just go right over, period. It doesn't even knock," said Waters.

"This reminds me," said the consultant, "of a mother who may want the kitchen to herself for a while, and suggests that her kid go try his new coloring book. The kid senses that this means that she wants room to prepare the dinner, so he sticks closer than ever to keep her from succeeding."

Everyone agreed, and laughed uncomfortably.

"This all reminds me," Gosling said, "of a friend of mine, a minister, who was out of work for a while. His wife told me she used to clean the house in an hour and a half, but with him there, it took her four hours. She couldn't bear having him around the house. They loved each other, of course, but she got really pissed off with him being there all the time."

This is the type of contribution which is likely to arise in a group and against which a consultant must guard, for by linking the case to the experiences of a fellow minister, it facilitates personal identification with the problem. The consultant correctly refused to follow this line of thought, and returned instead to close questioning of Waters's material.

"Are you pretty sure that there is suffering if the man comes back to an empty house?" the consultant asked.

"I'm pretty sure there is. This has always been the pattern."

"I'm wondering, you see, whether this is just his preference, or is he really miserable home alone, feeling neglected."

"This fellow loves reading, so he should be okay alone; but even when his wife goes to the store, he immediately puts on his coat to go too. He even insists on going with her to her needlework club. He sits in the background while the ladies gossip. His wife is terribly embarrassed, and the other women resent him—they can't talk freely with him around."

This produced great hilarity; and a curate gasped, "How can a tough, go-out-and-kill-'em executive behave like that? He must be crazy! Really masochistic. I mean, how can you believe that this guy has been traveling around for seventy-one years on somebody's apron strings? It sounds absolutely crazy."

"Maybe he wasn't," said the consultant quietly. "Maybe an equilibrium was held as long as the job was there, and it's now overbalanced."

"But, what I mean is, I can't believe this can go on forever!"

"Yes," said Waters, "but she is afraid that it will; she's looking into the future."

"Well," said the curate, "how do you see your role? How can you change the situation without taking sides? I'm quite sympathetic, but it looks to me as though nobody's getting the message—they're just breaking into factions."

"The interesting thing is," answered Waters, "that I can communicate with her, but I honestly cannot communicate with him. It's another one of these situations where you are talking, and there seems to be understanding. I even asked his advice about someone else's case that's similar to his own, then out he goes, into the same behavior."

"Perhaps," suggested Apple, "he's locked into his own expectations of what retirement would be. Perhaps his picture has been that he would no longer have to take any orders from anyone, and that he could now really live in the home he has supported for so many years."

"How does this sound to the rest of you?" asked the consultant. "Does this sound like a universal problem that we all
share? And in what way? And what can one do?"

This question was a major technical error. The consultant
was attempting to deal with a difficulty inherent in group consultation, how to make the discussion of one man's case relevant to the needs of other group members so that they will not
become mere observers. But by leaving the specific case and
inviting discussion of the issue in the abstract, and moreover,
by introducing the topic of expectations about retirement—an
ambiguous phrase that might refer to counseling problems, but
might equally be taken in a personal sense—as a "problem we
all share," he was inviting the group to leave the safety of the
displacement object, the case, and to express their own fears
and fantasies about retirement. This might have been acceptable in psychotherapy, but it is not advisable in consultation,
since it violates the rule that restricts discussion to issues of
professional functioning and to details of the client's case. This
was a particularly hazardous gambit in this group because the
preoccupation of several men with their own impending retirement was so close to the surface of consciousness; and uncovering it would probably have stirred up too much complicated
material for any clinician to contain in the remaining time
and in that setting, even assuming that this would have been
appropriate—which it was not.

The consultant's *faux pas* was met by utter silence. It was
broken by Mr. Philips, a young minister who had participated
in the consultation program for two years and who was consequently an experienced consultee. He ignored the psychiatrist's violation of decorum, and returned very firmly to the
case.

"What bothers me," he said, "is that I see everybody trying
to work on the husband, and I've yet to get the feeling that
he's at all upset about this. *She's* the one who's upset about it."

"You mean," said the consultant, "that everyone wants to change him to please her?"

"That's right," said Philips. "Here's a guy who has worked for forty-odd years; and now he's got a chance to do what he likes, and nobody's letting him do it!"

"Oh, he is doing it," said Waters, in a rising voice, stammering slightly. "The difficulty is——"

"To correct him!" shouted the curate.

Several people were talking at once, loudly, and there was rising nervous laughter.

"And your counter-proposal is what?" the consultant asked the curate.

"Well," began the young man.

"It would be hard to say," interjected Moss; and the level of laughter kept rising.

"I'm not sure exactly," said the curate, in a quieter tone. The quips and laughter redoubled. "The whole thing is crazy!" the young man continued. "I just can't believe it!" Among those now laughing hardest was the consultant.

Here we can see the group reacting, through raucous and inappropriate laughter, to the unbearable tension of finding themselves, like Waters, trapped in the case. They saw no apparent way to move without destroying one of the clients; and even if nothing changed, the wife would be smothered. The discussion so far, especially Apple's remark about the possible images a man might have of his own retirement, had intensified discomfort by making the man seem more sympathetic and, therefore, more vulnerable. Furthermore, the increasing vividness of the dilemma may have been impinging on the private concerns of some of those in the group.

"I'm very surprised at this reaction," broke in Waters. "Perhaps it's my special situation, but I'm surprised that more of you haven't been hearing from the wives."

"Not that way," answered Green. "My men seem to take off like a bat out of hell on all kinds of energetic trips when they retire, dragging protesting wives behind them."

Again the motif was emphasized of retirement as a state when one marriage partner was sacrificed to the needs of the other.

"Well, yes," said Waters, stammering, "but that's a different thing. I've got two or three cases where the husbands are home and the wives are going crazy. Wives want to know what to do with a husband that's retired."

This statement, which now places the case under discussion into a generally occurring category, marked another danger point, since it again diffused the focus of discussion and threatened to make someone think, "Perhaps I'm going to be like that—an unmanly, childlike burden on my wife, who will then resent and reject me." As long as the discussion was tied to the particular plight of Waters' parishioner, that danger was minimized.

"Well," said Moss, "I've certainly seen a good many husbands wear out a good many wives at retirement."

"The problem here seems to be that all this guy needs for happiness is one other person to go along with him. But she's younger, and she isn't about ready to retire herself," Griffin said.

"But she is going along," insisted Waters, "she's been capitulating all along. But she is getting more and more concerned each year about what this will lead to. It looks as though she's going to be *completely* caught in the house."

"If she's saying, 'The older my husband gets, the more I'll have to take care of him,' that's a real concern."

"I don't think she'd be concerned if this were a physical disability. But I think that she feels that she has to wear the pants in the whole situation, and she has no time that she can call her own."

"Then," said the consultant, "perhaps the focus should be on the wife—she is the one with problems, she is the one who's unhappy. He seems contented and to know what he wants."

"Yes," said Waters, "but he's manipulating her; and when she tries to share responsibility, he puts on the hurt or depressed situation, and she doesn't think it fair to shake him."

In this interplay, the consultant was trying to persuade the consultee that what he identified as the problem was not really critical, and that he should address himself instead to a different point; and Waters was correctly refusing to be moved. The consultant was saying, the husband is happy, the wife has a problem. The consultee, however, was concerned about the behavior of the husband, which he was determined to understand, and he was not willing to dismiss it.

"She feels she's got another child!"

"But there's no solid evidence yet that his age is a factor in this?"

"No, his health is fine."

"Maybe she's manipulated him into this situation and now doesn't like it," Philips suggested.

"No," Waters insisted, "she isn't that type. I don't think it's a case of a dominant wife who has subjugated her husband."

"Of course," said White, "it's possible that his social life had always been part of his business; and when he retired, he lost all of that."

"Yes," said Apple, "you often hear someone complaining that he doesn't have friends of his own. There are only his wife's friends and business contacts, but no personal attachments."

"It seems to me," said the consultant, "that for either one of these people to get what he wants, it's going to be a loss for the other."

Now the wise-cracking and raucous laughter began again and rose higher and higher. Someone, for example, suggested that this man had "retired with a vengeance." Another said, "It's impossible—old dogs, new tricks, you know; it's a charming challenge, Joe, but I'm glad it's *your* case." The consultant had now underlined and sanctioned the growing fear of the group that this was indeed a hopeless situation.

"But is it that hopeless?" the consultant wondered.

"From her point of view it could be," Green said.

"It's getting to be a threat for her," Waters said firmly. "She was in my office a couple of days ago, we talked about this."

"Was he waiting outside?"

"No, as a matter of fact, he was sleeping late that morning."

"So she does get away some," Moss said hopefully.

Waters sighed.

"Looking at it from his point of view," said White, the oldest member of the group, "I have a feeling that there's a great deal of sympathy for the wife here, but not too much for him. I can *feel* that situation in my own retirement that's coming up. The parish is taken away; you have to move out somewhere else; you have no friends. Who do you have left? You have nobody but your wife left."

"Yes," said Waters, "clergy retirement is another, most interesting thing, because you are a figure in a community; and when you retire to another community, where you're not an authority figure, that puts you in a John Doe situation, to say nothing of getting reacclimated."

"So," said the consultant, desperately trying to climb back on the case, "part of his way of acclimatizing was by saying that since he was somebody before retirement, and nobody now, he can sell magazine subscriptions, and that's good enough for him."

"We were speaking of clergy," said Waters nervously. "In the case of that retired man, I don't know if that's the case."

"It could be," said White. "I mean, everyone isn't going to retire at once. You do it one at a time. It's like dying. And so you're in a new role, and there's nobody there that you know. The other people remain on the job, and you . . . you're retired. So you have nobody but your wife; and if she's not prepared to play that part with you, you . . . you've got a problem."

"Yes," agreed the consultant, tossing all discretion and disciplined methods to the wind, "an ordinary man only works for eight hours a day, but you're a clergyman all twenty-four hours. It must be far worse for clergymen to retire."

This, of course, was a foolish move. Instead of helping a consultee who was having difficulty with a case because of some personal link between it and his own life to gain mastery by learning to treat such cases objectively, by strengthening the boundary between private and professional existence, the consultant was tearing at whatever shreds of a boundary were left. He was encouraging the ministers to look at their own fears of retirement, rather than helping them to manage the case of a retired man in the practice of one of their colleagues. Had the latter task been accomplished successfully, it might have had a secondary benefit in relieving a measure of those very fears in themselves. For, if this parishioner and his wife could be helped to establish a mutually satisfying, rather than a mutually destructive, experience, then these clergy in their own retirements might find a similarly happy lot. As soon as the consultant realized that the discussion was veering into dangerous waters, he should have pulled it back to the case, and held it there. Instead, he became so upset by the intimate disclosures and clear identification of some of the men with Waters' parishioner that he contributed to the very situation he knew must be avoided.

Fortunately, there were veteran consultees in the group; and as the consultant broke the rules, they set the situation right. This is one of the advantages of group over individual consultation. Groups are more complicated, but they are safer, since this kind of lapse by the consultant can be absorbed and recovered from relatively easily, as long as the ground rules of consultation have been properly understood and accepted by most of the consultees.

After a stunned silence and then more nervous laughter, therefore, Waters said briskly, "Well, come up with some answers, boys. I want help on this."

"I don't know what to do," said Griffin, "but I have the feeling *she's* the one . . ."

"Sure she is," Waters said, "all right! But the point is, what does she do? Where does she go? She has the problem, but she doesn't want any hurt here."

"Does he think that perhaps you're her mouthpiece?" asked a very perceptive minister.

"I've tried to approach this diplomatically, but he just doesn't seem to realize what a burden he is. I've tried to get this across to him, but . . . I feel for the wife, because I think she's fair, asking for some independence."

"I'm not so sure," Apple said.

"What?"

"I'm not so sure it is a fair thing to ask for."

"But what she wants is almost the same kind of sharing you get in normal life. What he has done is retire from all decision-making. He's retired from everything. I've known them for twenty years. They weren't like this before," said Mr. Waters.

"But he doesn't see this as a problem. Only she sees it as a problem."

"But the point is she can't get it across to him that it *is* a problem for her."

"Is this affecting her health?" the consultant asked.

"No. But she is worried about the future, that as he gets older, she'll be more and more tied down."

"If nothing changes, if it gets no better or worse, what will it cost her?" the consultant asked.

"Just the feeling that it's pinning her into a tighter sphere, and that she will be kept from her friends and interests. She realizes that with the age difference, if things don't improve now, they never will. And the way he follows her to her club meetings—that's creating tension in the group that's wearing her down. There's no divisiveness that's apparent between the husband and wife, though, because she holds back on discussing the issues so as not to hurt him."

"Can't she insist that some of her engagements are for women only?"

"No. That would create distrust."

The entire situation was summarized and chewed over twice more, and then, fortunately, the time was up. The consultant noted in a puzzled tone, "You've given us a lot of material. We've checked and rechecked until it's shiny-clear, but the group just can't seem to get on top of this one. Let's think about it for another time."

The meeting broke up, amid more inappropriate laughter.

The session floundered mainly because the clergy and the consultant largely failed to isolate the key factors in Waters's difficulty with the case. They did not deal with the fact that the presenter was regarding the husband not as a real person, with recognizable feelings which could be explored and changed, but as a stereotype, a creature apart, with whom neither his wife nor the clergyman could ever communicate. Here was a man who "has no abilities or interest," "who doesn't enjoy his grandchildren," who was so hurt when his wife left him alone that he accompanied her to the grocery shop and her sewing club like a clinging three-year-old, and who yet remained perversely contented with his lot. The man, Waters insisted, did not see a problem. He sat in the house, like a block of wood, reading novels or sleeping, oblivious to his wife's growing sense of being trapped and to the unseemliness of his own behavior. The act of speaking to him was particularly hazardous, and was regarded with almost superstitious awe. Nobody dared to risk hurting or depressing him, so everyone plotted how to manipulate him into a more acceptable form of behavior without having to face him directly.

The consultation group, with the exception of some isolated remarks from the curate and Apple, simply adopted Waters' stereotype, perhaps convinced of its accuracy by Waters' refusal to be moved from his view of the problem and by his consequent repetition of the elements of the case. The consultant himself was carried away, partly, he later said, because he thought that since Waters was such a wise and intelligent man, his perceptions must be accurate. He forgot that if the minister had been able to bring all his wisdom and intelligence to bear on the case, he would not have needed consultation. The consultant was also preoccupied with the fact that fear of retirement, or of losing their jobs because of parish politics, was close to the surface of group consciousness, and, indeed, was manifested on a number of occasions, aided by the consultant's self-fulfilling prophecy, in which he contributed actively to what he feared by linking these issues to the personal, rather than the professional experience of group members.

The only people in the room who seemed at ease with the case were the curates and two or three younger men. The rest of the group, however, consistently rode over the latters' suggestions which said, "But this man can't be as you describe him." When, for example, a curate roared with laughter at the idea of a man accompanying his wife to a ladies' club meeting, and said, "I can't believe that a seventy-year-old executive could really be like that," he was ignored by his colleagues, who were wedded, by then, to Waters' characterization. They were also reacting, incidentally, to a note of discourtesy in the young man's remarks, which the group refused to tolerate. When Apple spoke up on the side of the husband, conveying the possible meaning of retirement as a time when a man no longer has to take orders and when he can at last enjoy the home he has supported over the years, it was never picked up because, by then, the whole current of the meeting was flowing in the opposite direction. Had the consultant been more objective at this moment, he could have seized on Apple's point to help Waters reconsider the husband in a more human light; but the consultant was as trapped by the case as were most of the ministers. By this time, he was also relating to it personally rather than professionally, for as he admitted later, "It got me, too. I was thinking about my father's recent retirement."

In the absence of adequate objectivity on the part of the consultant, the entire group not only adopted Waters's stereotyped perceptions, but began to act out his dilemma. Everyone talked about the retired man just as Waters and the wife had done, trying to find ways of manipulating this inert mass for his own good and that of his wife; and they thereby adopted all the premises which blocked prospects for success. The discussion ran in ever tighter circles, reemphasizing the inherent hopelessness of the case. The consultant tried to extricate himself on two or three occasions, suggesting that present conditions might continue but not deteriorate, and implying that if so, the wife could tolerate them. This, however, was not received with much enthusiasm amid the general gloom of the discussion.

On considering the case later, however, the consultant realized that Waters had unconsciously set up a syllogism in his own mind which was blocking his handling of the problem. This syllogism seemed to say: a man whose relations with people have depended on his role, as does that of an executive (and also that of a clergyman), is likely, after retirement, to grow dependent on his wife. He then becomes like a child; and she must either accept him as a burden, giving up her own independence, or reject him. Either way, one of the parties must lead an intolerable existence that can only deteriorate further as the years pass.

Since all the participants in the group came to accept Waters' basic premises, the discussion focused on trying to find some less catastrophic outcome to the situation. And since this was impossible, given the terms of the argument, the tension of the group rose higher and higher, to be relieved periodically in high-pitched, nervous laughter, whenever it became particularly clear that however the minister might turn, either the man or his wife was bound to be injured. The group found itself obliged either to accept the wife's position or to attack her.

Either they had to contemplate punitive action against the husband, with whom at least some of the group identified as potentially retired men themselves who would be left with only their wives for company, or they had to hurt the woman by supporting the husband's hostile dependence. Some, however, may also have identified with the wife, as the burden carrier who cannot complain openly but whose independence is sacrificed to the unjustified demands of others. So her plight was especially painful for them to contemplate.

One way to break through this impasse would have been to discuss barriers to communication. Waters might then have been urged to see that although this man had become socially isolated and idle because of retirement from his profession, and consequently driven into exaggerated dependence on his wife, nevertheless, as a mature person, he must be expected to confront and work through his difficulties. With the minister's help, the couple might have been brought to accommodate themselves to each other; but this would not be likely to occur if the husband were dismissed as an obstinate child, or regarded as so vulnerable that it would be perilous to talk to him. Waters might have been helped to consider the case as one in which marital counseling was required, where he would meet with both parties together to ease their communication.

Further, it might have been suggested that Waters help the wife to develop a more realistic appraisal of her husband and his capabilities so that her expectations of tragedy might have been modified. Since the husband was so much older than the wife, a fact whose significance seemed to elude all but the curate, throughout her married life she might have dreaded the prospect of his one day sinking into helpless dependence. She might have molded his recent behavior unconsciously by this expectation, creating a self-fulfilling prophecy. And she may have actually exaggerated his dependence by her defensive rejection, like a mother who tries to free herself from a child's demands, only to precipitate more whining and clinging.

The consultant might have broadened the discussion to explore certain complexities of interpersonal relations which arose from this case. For example, he might have spoken of the obstacles to the minister's free and trusting relationship with one spouse if he spends most of his time with the other; for it was clear in retrospect that Waters was getting almost all of his information from the wife, and was directing most of his sympathy at her. Consequently, his view of the husband after knowing him for twenty years was distorted by the wife's bias. And since in any family conflict there may be discrepancies between the parties in their perceptions and expectations of each other, a mediator should not jump to the conclusion that any one story epitomizes objective reality.

That this issue really needed general discussion was borne out some weeks later when a young minister mentioned in passing that he had been told by a female parishioner of her husband's cruelty. The clergyman later learned from a psychologist who was treating another member of the family that the woman's version of the matter was highly distorted. The clergyman said that he then felt betrayed by his parishioner— by the way in which, he thought, she had elicited his sympathy under false pretenses; and he concluded that she was far too disturbed for him to help. It did not seem to occur to him to call in the husband to try to resolve some of the contradictions between the two stories. The minister had no doubt been taught in theory what to do in marital counseling, but under the pressure of a complex case, he forgot to apply what he had learned. The consultation session, therefore, provided an opportunity to make existing theoretical knowledge vital by pinning it to a flesh-and-blood situation.

The ministers might have been warned against the possibility of a coalition developing between one spouse and the clergyman in which they line up against the other spouse. The pastor would then serve not as a communication bridge between the conflicting factions, as he had intended, but would,

rather, draw them further apart by supporting one person in
being separate from the other by repeatedly concurring in a
partisan view. Thus, inadvertently, Waters might have been
strengthening the wife's conception of her husband as stubborn
and hopeless, and may thereby have contributed to her belief
that this burden would ruin her life.

Since such inadvertent collusion would be likely to color
any contacts between Waters and the husband, the man
would probably sense a lack of sympathy in the minister, despite the fact that the latter was genuinely trying to help him.
The retired man, therefore, might have dug in his heels further
to resist the pressure that he felt to be directed toward the exclusive benefit of his wife. In this way, the clergyman might
have been creating a self-fulfilling prophecy. Because he was
convinced of the man's obduracy, he might have communicated his irritation and pushed too hard, thus rousing further
stubbornness in the man, which in turn supported the precon-
ceptions of the wife and Waters. The consultant might have
suggested that ministers guard against this by interviewing
both spouses together from the early stages of a case in order
not only to obtain some realistic assessment of the facts, and to
identify and mediate those divergent perceptions which would
emerge in face-to-face meetings, but also to demonstrate to parishioners their own friendly neutrality. In Waters' case, on
the other hand, where the minister might already be identified
by the husband as the wife's ally, the rector might have
brought in other mediators, whose disinterestedness was assured, to redress the balance.

In this connection, the consultant might have suggested ex-
tending the case's focus, when assessing and treating the problem, to include all the relevant members of the clients' network. Waters had neglected the potential contribution of the
couple's grown children. Apple, in his story of his uncle's retirement, recommended precisely this approach of gathering
those who are close to the couple in order both to dilute the in-

tensity of a situation and to sanction a solution which the couple alone might have thought to be forbidden. This also could have been managed with the help of others in the parishioners' lives, such as a family doctor, a neighbor, or any one of a wide group of possible intercessors who can usually be found once the minister realizes the importance of mobilizing them.

The consultant's performance on this occasion had been well below his usual level of professional activity. Puzzled by this, and feeling foolish, he sought the advice of a colleague, as is customary among psychiatrists when they meet with confusing cases. Now the minister's consultant had himself assumed the role of consultee; and in reexamining Waters' account of his parishioners, and the course of the group's discussion with his own consultant, the psychiatrist came to realize that his view of the material had been constrained. The second psychiatrist suspected that personal concerns ("I kept thinking of my own father's retirement") had clouded his colleague's professional judgment. He kept his interpretations to himself, however, since his friend had come to him for consultation, not for psychotherapy; and, instead, he tactfully pointed to data which suggested alternate ways by which the circumstances of Waters' parishioners and the course of the ministers' discussion might have been modified. He helped his consultee to distance himself from the material—to reinforce the boundary between his private and professional lives—with the hope that this renewed objectivity would carry over to other cases of like nature in the future.

Despite the shortcomings of this session, there were some modest gains. Waters showed a certain sardonic satisfaction in the fact that his case had so completely puzzled the group; and he may have concluded that he was not, on reflection, as inept as he had thought. Indeed, the discussion seemed to ease his feelings and to suggest some new ideas; for a couple of weeks later, he reported that the husband was not quite such a problem any more. Waters had talked him into attending the church's retired men's club, and he hoped to expand the man's activities even further.

Thus this particular case was eased by the simple fact of sharing it with sympathetic colleagues. Few gains, however, can have been made in educating Waters and the other ministers to human-relations issues arising out of it which could be generalized to future cases. It also failed to weaken Waters' subjective involvement with cases of this category in order to strengthen his professional poise or to alleviate the fear of some of the group members about the imagined horrors of their own impending retirement. It did, however, teach the consultant that the distorting power of his own subjective reactions should be guarded against as carefully in this type of work as in psychotherapy.

chapter 5

A Successful Case—
Part I: Unfolding

The failure of the consultation process in Waters' case, summarized in the preceding chapter, was encouraged further by the way in which the psychiatrist and the group attempted to deal with the material in only one session. While it is possible to offer help on some circumscribed matters in a short time, complex cases and deeply rooted blind spots not unnaturally require far more effort and thought. The better a consultant knows his consultee, and the more he learns about the case, the more likely he will be to identify his problem. And since he is not a mind reader, it may take two or three sessions before he has amassed sufficient evidence to see the salient issues and before he can intervene forcefully and directly enough to modify a consultee's settled ways of looking at a particular situation.

The consultee also needs time: first, to build up sufficient confidence in the consultant and the group to reveal the extent of his own perplexity; second, to sort out the details of his case until enough order is established for the few apparently insoluble points to be isolated; and third, to digest and react to the consultant's and the group's suggestions. This latter point is of particular significance, since to experience the greatest benefit the consultee must move back and forth between the theoretical formulations of the consultation setting and the untidy realities of his parish work. Only by returning to the actual case to test the wisdom of the group's suggestions, and by then analyzing the results in subsequent sessions, can a consultee ensure that these ideas are worth his serious attention; and only in this way can he fully assimilate a novel point of view.

Let us examine another case, therefore, in which a less hurried approach, coupled with better technique on the part of the psychiatrist, yielded more satisfying results.

Mr. Philips, a young minister with a charming manner, was a veteran consultee. In his comments on the cases of others, and in anecdotes about his own parish, he sounded flexible and imaginative, always revealing a warm, nurturing attitude even toward more conservative or eccentric parishioners. Nevertheless, the consultant had noticed that Philips had a tendency to seek out and react allergically to "castrating bitches," even when evidence for the existence of such creatures in a particular case was slight. When this minister offered to present a case, therefore, the consultant had these points in mind.

Two weeks earlier, Philips began, a middle-aged parishioner had summoned the minister to his house in the early morning to talk to his wife. When Philips arrived, he had found the woman huddled on her bedroom floor in an acute state of anxiety. This had startled him, since he had known her for some years as an unusually active member of his congregation, a woman who was able to manage capably a house, a part-time job, voluntary activities, and the care of four children, the two youngest of whom were in primary school, and the eldest, a seventeen-year-old girl, handicapped by polio since infancy, who was largely confined to a wheelchair. Philips had seen the woman a week earlier when she had addressed a church meeting, and he had noticed no sign of strain. He now learned that she had been trying to write a term paper for an extension course at a local college when she became paralyzed by terror. Philips had spent four hours calming the woman and coaxing her off the floor. He had seen her every day since, first at her house and then at his office, but he felt no improvement in her condition.

"When I just talk to Jane," Philips said, "she immediately thinks of a number of things she cannot do. And I just feel, as I sit in a room with her, and she begins listing the things she can't do, my insides just . . . I almost feel like saying something like 'Boy, it sure does sound like you can't do a damned thing!' "

The consultant saw that some aspect of the case had struck Philips on a raw nerve. The psychiatrist jumped to no conclusions, however; he merely asked for more information.

Philips continued: "I can picture dealing with this person for some time, and . . . there's not enough money for psychiatry. My lady did go to the local mental health center, but a neighbor of Jane's saw her going in, and she gossips. Now there's another complication—Jane has an appointment next week with the social worker there about her daughter. The center is trying to involve parents of handicapped children, and she doesn't want to go because she doesn't like the counselor. As far as I can make out, the counselor got impatient with my lady and tried to push her into doing more for her daughter.

"Then, on Monday, I went to the house and saw the daughter, because the girl had said, 'Can I talk to you, because my mother gives me hell all the time?' . . . I just wondered if any of you guys run into this kind of thing. My long-term concern is, this is something I'm going to have to take care of. I repeat, there's no money for a psychiatrist!"

As the discussion progressed, it appeared that Philips had become so caught in the case that any recital of the parishioner's circumstances only brought him back to his own feelings of worry and perplexity. However the consultant and the group maneuvered, the consultee's level of tension would not come down.

In his daily meetings with Jane, Philips had amassed a vast and dismal array of details about her situation, about her contempt for her own abilities and her resentment of her crippled daughter; about her fear-ridden childhood, dominated by a father who allowed no failures; and about her current existence—obsessed by her struggle to maintain a middle-class, suburban façade with too little money and a husband who could never advance in his job far enough to fulfill her ambitions. Despite his intelligence and psychological sophistication, however, Philips seemed too inhibited, for reasons of his own, to draw this material into a usable pattern, and it remained for him a menacing labyrinth in which he felt entangled and trapped.

Waters realized the problem at once. "Do I hear you saying," he asked, "that you are over your head dealing with this person? That you think the case is going to get too much for you to handle?"

Before the consultant could intervene, Philips had answered, "The first time I saw her, her husband was there. The second time, it really was a case of estimating whether this was over my head. I distinctly remember feeling that I couldn't stop her from compounding the kinds of things she could not do. So I suppose part of the difficulty was evaluating whether or not it was over my head. But . . . I think I voted, 'No, it is not.' "

Significantly, the case had not seemed so formidable with someone else present. But when Philips had faced Jane and her sense of inadequacy alone, he had had an irrational urge to escape. Nevertheless, he persisted as though drawn to and fascinated by the situation, convinced that in the absence of a real psychiatrist, he was obligated to play the psychiatric role. He began to mimic psychotherapeutic techniques, setting himself to uncover and challenge Jane's feelings. He sensed the danger and futility of this, however, for throughout he kept wondering whether he was damaging her.

"What was Jane's major concern?" the consultant asked, drawing the discussion away from a direct review of Philips' own doubts, while opening a path to discovering issues that rendered this case so threatening for the consultee.

"She was taking a night-school course," the minister explained, "which was proving too difficult for her. It is part of a degree program she's been in for three years. She had wanted to take an easier course, but a friend had persuaded her to take this one instead. She didn't like the course, and she had to produce a paper, and she could not write. She was so tense and nervous that she could not apply her mind to the material. She kept insisting that she had to keep on taking the course. She said, 'I'd like to drop out, but if I do, I might not have the determination to continue next spring; then I know I'll be dropped from the program.' Then she said, 'I won't finish! I won't be able to do it!' So I asked her, 'Why is school so important to you?' And she said, 'I don't know; I feel I've got to produce.'

" 'Well, what do you have to produce?'

" 'I don't know, I just have to be in this course!' "

Philips, who was now acting Jane's part by his posture and by the changing inflections of his voice, explained that the woman was afraid that if she were dropped from school for failing to take the prescribed number of courses each term, she would lose all the credits she had earned over the past three years. If she continued, however, she would have to work for nine more years before she got her degree.

"What a depressing prospect!" exclaimed a member of the group.

"I also found out," Philips continued, "that she constantly compares herself with others and thinks she's inferior to them. So she has to take courses that are too hard for her because otherwise she thinks her friends will look down on her."

The minister's attitude was of exasperation jostling sympathy—exasperation at Jane's apparent determination to persist in an absurd and untenable position. This created a sense of impasse, since all appeals to reason and self-interest were ignored.

"What about her husband?" asked Moss.

"He's an assistant manager in a local plant; nothing spectacular. She says, 'I've always pushed him, and he finally admitted that it was good that I pushed him, because he never would have done so well without being pushed.' "

From this remark and related ones made throughout the session, the consultant understood that one aspect of Philips' difficulty came from his ambivalence toward Jane. On the one hand, he pitied her suffering; and whenever he suspected that she had been attacked, as at the counseling center, he spoke of her as "my lady." But this was counterbalanced by disgust at what he perceived as her bitchiness—her driving of her husband and herself, her grasping after social status, and her "frivolous" complaints about the superficial deprivations of her life. Philips' possible identification with Jane's sense of inadequacy only strengthened his dislike, forming a defense against complaints that might have been unwelcome reminders of problems of his own. The consultant, therefore, decided that one goal of the session must be to modify Philips' stereotypes in order to detach him from identification with the case, and thereby reduce his confusion, anxiety, and guilt about his hostility to Jane.

"But the husband hasn't done well," Green pointed out.

"No," Philips agreed. "And this is a constant illustration of the things she has tried to do and has never been able to get any satisfaction from. I began to see pretty clearly that she would *never* see that she was satisfied. She set out to do this twelve-year course because it was impossible to get any satisfaction out of that, and she would have to keep on struggling, and hating the courses, and never achieve anything. This was the kind of hole she began to dig for me. As I speak this, you can all begin to feel, 'What can I say?' that kind of response."

Philips clearly foresaw an inevitably hopeless outcome for the case, since all its constituent parts were so bleak. This assured him that his own efforts to help Jane would be blocked at every turn.

After further questions, however, Philips did begin to acknowledge, albeit grudgingly, that Jane was functioning remarkably well despite her claims to be weak and incompetent. Her house was immaculate, her children well behaved, and it emerged in an aside that during the past six months she had suffered the deaths of her mother and sister without giving way to the strain. She and her husband were well established in the community.

"They pioneered in this area," Philips said, "and now, as she puts it, 'Everyone has gone by us.' Their friends have moved up and on to higher-class places; and they've been left."

"Is she likable?" Apple asked.

"Very likable—on the surface. I think," Philips continued after a pause, "that she feels that she's always got to be around to take care of the paralyzed child."

"How seriously is the girl disabled?" the consultant asked.

"She's in a wheelchair most of the time. I've just learned that she was living down in the basement, and she's only been upstairs for the last few months."

"Living in the basement?" the consultant asked.

"Yes," said Philips in a strained voice. "I couldn't help the immediate thought that rushed through my mind: 'Boy, you kept her in a hole! You kept her down there!' "

"Sometimes a basement is part of the living area of the house," the consultant said.

Philips quickly agreed. "I'm sure they made plenty of accommodations for her to be comfortable. The mother was telling me about this because she was complaining about the finish being scratched off the furniture all over the house by the wheelchair. I mumbled something like, 'Well, it's good to

have Patricia upstairs even if the furniture does get damaged.'
I have the feeling that the care of her daughter upsets her very
much. There's a constant demand there."

Here Philips's ambivalence was amplified. The bitch motif
was growing stronger, but coexisted with the minister's sympathy for Jane's depression at being tied to the care of a chronic
invalid.

"Is it your judgment that this seventeen-year-old doesn't
need an adult in the house all the time?" the consultant asked.
Where, in other words, are the realistic boundaries of Jane's
burden? This introduced the idea that even such long-term responsibilities may vary in intensity over time, and need not
sap the life of the caregiver. This point was explicitly applied
to Jane, but it had implicit significance for Philips too, since
he perceived a commitment to help this parishioner as invaria-
bly all-absorbing.

"It was my feeling that the mother ought to trust the girl
more," Philips said. "The girl doesn't have friends of her own
age. What I learned from the girl was that the deaths of the
grandmother and the aunt were catastrophic for her. She pre-
fers older people, and she obviously has a conflict with her
mother."

"What about this counselling service?" the consultant
asked. "How long has Jane been going?"

"She's just started," Philips answered.

"Who got her in? Why did she go?"

"I don't know. . . . It's a good question. I suspect, since it's
connected with her daughter, that it was the school."

"What's the problem with the neighbor seeing her?" the
consultant asked.

"She gossips," Philips said.

"So what? What was there to say?" To this Philips did not
seem prepared to answer.

"Some people are ashamed to be seen going through the
door of such places," White said.

"Jane whispers in my office," Philips whispered urgently, as though he were revealing a sinister detail. "There was nobody around on the floor, though you could hear people coming and going downstairs, but she whispered!"

"Was she whispering, no matter what she talked about?" the consultant asked calmly, restoring a tone of analytical detachment.

"She whispered all the time," Philips answered. "She was just so afraid that somebody else would hear her talk about her problem. Her image of herself is terribly important."

The minister seemed to see Jane's sensitivity as further confirmation that she could not be helped. It proved that defense of her self-image, of her "suburban façade," would prevent her from ever exposing the extent of her difficulties even to herself and her pastor. Consequently, she would keep inaccessible the key to a disturbance that was disrupting not only her own life, but also those of her husband and children, and thus willfully and absurdly resist measures that might ease her suffering. So, in accepting the responsibility for her care, Philips saw himself trapped more tightly than ever in a hopeless case; if it were not inherently hopeless, which for some reason he believed it to be, her resistance would make it so.

"It sounds so sad," Apple said. "She sounds like a terribly frustrated woman who has visions of grandeur, and who can't possibly achieve them. She tries to take courses so that she will have a college diploma like other women she knows and be able to get a glamorous job someday: but she's still tied to this family situation, so no amount of effort will do her any good. She's living in your area, which is an on-the-way-up community, full of young executive types. She hasn't much money and probably won't ever have any. She'd do well to move somewhere else if her husband is going to have a low-level job for the rest of his life. She's going to see these things around her till the day she dies."

"What I'd like to do is to help her to see that she's worth

something as a person," Philips said without conviction.

The consultant, following Apple's humanizing interpretation of traits that Philips had been describing as perverse, yet trying to minimize the global pessimism of his remarks, said, "It sounds as though something has recently upset Jane's image of herself: and she seems to have a self-image that requires an awful lot of effort to sustain. Could she feel that she's been scolded at the counseling center for failing in her mothering role? Did the counselor get at her about the basement? And then, did all the worries about money, and so on, loom up? If the whispering meant shame and guilt, could it date back to the discovery that her child would be handicapped, and the mother thinking that the girl caught polio because she didn't care for her properly? Are shame and guilt now being stirred up by contact with that center? And then, you've got her father's refusal to tolerate failure, so when things go awry, she feels responsible."

"One thing more," White said, "she's going through the menopause. Over the years with this group," he added firmly, "I've learned the importance of the menopause." The consultant seemed taken aback. "I mean," White continued, "women feel they're not functioning in that area, so they feel they're not functioning in any other area either."

"Also," Waters said, "as she considers her own resentment against her daughter, who keeps her from doing things, there's a guilt that develops——"

"She says," Philips interrupted, with intense feeling, " 'I don't want to hate my daughter!' "

Throughout the session, with the group's help, Philips was able to build the vast tangle of details of the case into a pattern for the first time. When alone, the material had apparently been too confusing and upsetting to examine closely. For since the consultee was convinced, for reasons which were still not clear, that Jane's situation was hopeless and destructive to those around her, he was afraid of finding these forebodings

confirmed. Within the relative safety of the consultation setting, however, even if the minister were to discover a monster
at the heart of the labyrinth, he would have allies to support
him. He would not have to deal with the danger alone. So now
he was prepared to consider a factor he found shocking, the
full intensity of Jane's hostility toward her child.

"She must think of her daughter as a great big roadblock,"
said Apple gently.

"A millstone," Philips agreed. "The girl was hospitalized for
a long time, and that used up a fantastic amount of money.
And now Jane has to pay for counseling. She said to me, 'If I
hear my daughter's name again, I think I'm going to scream!'
Those were her very words, 'If I hear her name, I'll scream!'
To me that meant, 'Everyone's interested in my daughter, but
they're not interested in me.' "

"When did she say that?" the consultant asked, taking note
of Philips's conflicting identifications, both with the mother
and the daughter.

"She said it when I first came in. That was one of the early
statements, when she was most distraught."

"I don't know how this fits the experience of the rest of
you," the consultant said, "but according to mine, families of
handicapped children come to some level of adjustment when
the kids are much younger than this girl is now. It may not be
a comfortable feeling, but it usually has a steadiness. Either
the lady has never acquired this; or something has given the
relationship a real shake. It might have been the appointments
at the counseling center, or it might be something else."

"You're talking about accommodating to realities," Moss
asked, "and admitting, 'This is where we are'?"

"Right," the consultant said. "Acknowledging reality and
realizing that the bitter kernel of it isn't going to change."

"You mean," Philips said, "that they learn what she can do,
what she can't do, what we'll trust her with, whether she can
dress herself, whether she can be left to take care of the

younger children? That sort of thing?"

"That sort of thing," the consultant agreed. "They learn it, they learn to accept it, and they weave it into the rest of the family life."

"You know," said Moss, "it strikes me that the thoughts and feelings that she expresses are not all that bad or unusual."

"I agree," the consultant said. "Here's someone who up till two weeks ago seemed in perfectly good shape. She'd come through two funerals, she's been carrying those extension courses for three years, she runs a house well, she participates in church groups, and she handles a handicapped kid plus the little ones more or less adequately. That's quite a record."

"Two weeks ago," Philips agreed, "I would not have suspected that anything was wrong." He still sounded puzzled and unhappy.

"All right," said the consultant, "what happened? What triggered the crisis? Things like this don't come out of the blue, there has to be a reason behind it all."

"I notice," Waters said, "that she's had two babysitters taken from her in the persons of the grandmother and the aunt. That may have taken away some of her feeling of being able to cope."

"That's possible," Philips admitted. "The girl used to stay with her grandmother for weeks at a time."

"We seem to have been exploring two possibilities," the consultant said. "First, that Jane has been accumulating pressures for years until a final straw broke the camel's back; second, that something very particular and new happened recently to upset everything. Taking the first alternative," he continued, "is it possible that she has been carrying that social status business, and the money problem, the handicapped youngster, several other things and the stress of the extension courses, and she could carry the whole lot as long as nothing more was added? Then, a relatively small thing tipped the balance. 'The last straw' is a real phenomenon. People can carry three or four loads, then the fifth, which may be trivial, tips everything over."

"You said something," Philips interrupted, "about being able to accommodate to having a handicapped child?"

"The balance of that might have been upset by something," the consultant explained, "like appointments at the center."

"It's possible that that counseling upset things," Philips mused.

"This business of the guilt," said Green, "and this feeling that if she hears the name of her child once more, she's going to climb the walls——"

"Makes me feel mad at her!" interrupted Moss.

"It doesn't me at all, because I don't see this as being terribly abnormal," Green continued. "I've heard this sort of thing many times. But I think it's crushing to her self-image, the fact that she feels this way."

Here members of the group expressed and answered an unspoken sentiment of Philips'. The latter, like Moss, resented the mother's resentment of her daughter. In doing so, he was relinquishing professional objectivity and reacting like an ordinary bystander. Green was reestablishing a professional atmosphere of detached compassion which allowed for the vagaries of human nature; but he was correcting the atmosphere impersonally, without attacking Philips' position.

"I'm wondering," Green continued, "whether it might be helpful to discuss her feelings with her from the standpoint of 'That's really not so bad, Jane, to feel that way. It's a perfectly normal thing; you mustn't castigate yourself because you have these tremendous guilt feelings. These feelings are the result of some pretty logical thought processes.' "

"Maybe I can explore this whole area of how Jane has adjusted to the girl's illness," Philips agreed, seizing a concrete suggestion which fitted his own taste for psychological exploration so well.

"I'd be rather careful there. I'd keep the idea in my mind

that the crisis had something to do with the daughter, but I'm not sure I would say anything about it yet," the consultant said firmly. He was anxious to prevent Philips from engaging in any further explorations of his parishioner's raw feelings where he might rapidly move out of his depth. The psychiatrist, therefore, discouraged this suggestion despite its humane tone. In doing so he was acting as a mental health specialist, watching for forces that might endanger an already unstable personality; and hence he was prepared to veto inappropriate suggestions from the group.

Meanwhile, Philips had built up enough confidence to expose a further measure of his own ambivalence. "I didn't know what to say when she said that about not wanting to hear her daughter's name once more. I instinctively felt like using her name."

There was a shocked silence, and then the group laughed in sympathy.

"I did," Philips continued in a louder voice. "I had the instinctive gut feeling of saying——"

"Patricia!" someone said.

"Patricia!" Philips shouted. Everyone laughed uncomfortably, but nevertheless, by their understanding reaction, they helped Philips to express his hostility without shame.

"How long before she made that statement had she been to the counseling service?" Waters asked.

"She had *just* seen the counselor who didn't like her," Philips answered in a tone of dawning enlightenment. "And she was supposed to go back to talk about herself and her daughter."

"So, what she got from the session was criticism of herself, rather than the feeling that anyone was trying to help her?" the consultant asked.

"That's right. He gave her the feeling that she wasn't taking the girl out enough, especially to social occasions. Jane says, 'I can't take her. These affairs take place thirty miles away. I have to drive her there, wait for her, and bring her back; and it's one more thing that I have to do for her.' What she's afraid of is that the next session is for the parents, and they will tell her to do more and more."

"The mother may be responding just to the added demands on her time," White said. "I had a case like that recently in which the daughter had to be taken back and forth to the psychiatrist and to group-therapy sessions, and the mother simply didn't have any time."

"Time is a problem for Jane," Philips said. "She's one of those over-involved suburbanites. She's always rushing off to things; and if anyone asks her to do anything, she takes it on. She never gives herself any breathing space."

"I've got a woman like that in my parish," Moss said. "Whenever she gets into one of these panic states, she goes out and adds something else. It's almost a drive that they have to keep going and load up. This woman complains about not having enough time. She works, but she doesn't have enough time to work full-time, so she only works part-time; but she stays extra. Then, she has an extra job selling cosmetics in the neighborhood. She's on our Parish Council; she's doing this, she's doing that. Anyone asks her to do anything, she does it. She just piles herself up the devil of a mess, and all of a sudden, she comes tearing into my office, yelling, 'I can't do any more!' I talk to her for a while. And the next time I see her, she says, 'I just started this new project.' "

"Activity seems to be a high point in many people's lives," Philips said. "It seems to be hard for them to cut out activities. They feel they've failed."

"If people enter into a lot of activity in order to feel better about themselves, to bolster their self-image," the consultant explained, "then it backfires if they can't pull it off. The thing that makes a person load up like that is the same thing that makes her feel bad when she can't carry it all."

Everyone pondered the implications of that idea.

"In my general operations in the church," Philips said, "I have a terrible fear of asking people to do things, because I don't know if they really can handle the load. This is a real problem for me as a parish priest, because there are other people who are so lonely, who really need something like this. Now I never said to Jane, 'You ought to drop your church work.' But if she ever brought up the possibility, I would have said, 'That's all right.' But that would be terribly difficult, because even if the idea had come from her, I feel she would eventually blame me for it. I think churches often do harm to some people under the general philosophy that activity is good for them. Sometimes it just gives them too much to carry."

After the group had considered that remark in the context of their own parish organization, Waters recalled them to the case at hand,

"Would there be any wisdom in supporting the counseling service?"

"One of the things I've thought of doing was calling the counseling service and saying, 'Listen, *I'm* taking care of this deal,' which I could do," Philips said firmly.

"You could, of course," said Apple carefully. "But wouldn't it be good for her to keep on with them? Just because she feels frustrated and afraid with them doesn't necessarily mean that they are not on the right track."

"She might be facing things now," the consultant said, "that another family might have coped with ten or fifteen years earlier. And it's painful; no matter when you do it, it hurts, but the longer you wait, the worse it gets. Now, as I understand it, the counseling center is mainly for Patricia's benefit, isn't it? You are on the side of the mother, but they are working for the child. There might be some benefit in that."

Here, in other words, was a possible way around Philips' conflicting identifications with both Jane and her daughter, which should not be squandered.

"Do you know people at the center well enough to talk to

them about this? They may not even realize how shaken she has become after their worker talked to her," Moss said.

"Yes, I do know some of them," Philips answered. "And this has just come to me here and now, which is a very helpful thing—I now plan to approach these people and discuss the case with them without any preconceived notions of my taking the situation over."

"You need all the help you can get in a complicated case like this," Moss said. "There are medical issues to do with the girl. It's highly technical stuff."

"If you were to tell the counseling center that you are taking over, I don't see what that would gain you. It could lose you something," the consultant added.

"I had thought of doing that until today. Now I think I'll just contact them and see what they think."

"There is a question," Waters said quietly, "as to how long you do keep on with the case. You may reach a plateau when you don't feel that much is happening, and then it will be time to hand it on to others."

Philips brushed the suggestion aside, still unable to accept that others could assume a major role in Jane's care.

"How much support does Jane get from her husband?" the consultant asked, following the opening made by Waters. "He doesn't sound very prominent in all this."

"I think she gets a very naïve, everything-is-going-to-be-all-right kind of support at the moment. Overall, I think he just goes out to work and provides for his family. Actually, he's the one person I haven't really talked to . . . I don't know. . . . It would keep you busy to be married to a gal like that."

"I look at the basement situation differently," Waters said. "We had a time when our kids loved to live in the basement, and we felt it gave them far more freedom. So it could be looked at in two ways: either as a case of subjugating kids, or a case of releasing them."

"I must confess," Philips said, "I had an automatic response

GEG

that this girl was being shut away, and I hadn't thought of it from the point of view you've brought up."

"I don't know, of course," Waters added hastily. "It would depend on the child and her own feelings. But it should be taken into account before placing the finger of judgment on the mother."

Philips agreed.

"I wouldn't necessarily think of it as a bad arrangement," White continued, "just something different."

"This has been very helpful to me," Philips said emphatically, as the meeting ended.

"Perhaps," said the consultant, "we could discuss this again when you've had a chance to see more of this lady."

Besides helping Philips to piece the details of the case into some kind of recognizable pattern, the consultant felt that this session had begun to resolve the minister's conflicting feelings toward his parishioner. Since she appeared to him not only as a bitch, but as a vulnerable suffering bitch, who thereby engaged not only his hostility but also his compassion, Philips found himself in the untenable position of sympathizing both with Jane and with her "victims." This session had begun to chip away at these stereotypes and to create a healthy distance, based on dispassionate reasoning, between the minister and the family. The range of pressures on Jane had been explored, and her apparently petty or harsh demands on herself and her family were now seen to flow logically from poignant experiences.

The fact that Philips was beginning to see Jane as a real, suffering human being, however, *raised* his level of anxiety, for now the cost of failure—with failure itself a sensitive issue—was increased. If the minister could convince himself that Jane were indeed a bitch, then failing to help her would be painful but endurable. But if the parishioner were found to be a likable woman after all, who had been struggling bravely for years to maintain herself and her family despite reverses, then his failure would be unendurable.

The group had only started to tackle the question of whether anyone else shared in Jane's care and whether others, in consequence, bore with Philips responsibility for the outcome of the case. Here the group insisted firmly that the minister not exclude the counseling service, but rather, that he join forces with its staff. They also tried to curb his zeal for psychiatric explorations, at least until more was known about Jane's condition. Finally, Philips was encouraged to consider the role of the husband in easing the woman's condition.

Despite an active discussion, in which much material was sifted, the consultant still had only the dimmest idea of what specifically made this case so onerous for Philips, and why he felt driven to expend such large amounts of time and energy on a situation which appalled him. The help that the group had extended so far had affected only the surface. The core problem would not appear until much later in the consultation process.

Had the discussion of Philips' case ended here, there would have been almost no enduring gains. The next meeting, held two weeks later, showed that there had been much backsliding in the consultee's attitudes. His tension and despondency had been renewed and strengthened after further contact with the case and after the support of the group had been found to produce no ready answers to Jane's misery.

"This, you may remember," Philips said, "is the case of the woman who dropped out of her extension course and needed some handholding. Her suburban façade is cracking open. You remember, she has a crippled child, and she alternates between not being able to touch her daughter and feelings of pressure that she has to take her everywhere.

"I asked her about the history of the handicap, and she said that the illness occurred when the girl was two. When she was about ten, she had a series of operations to make her walk, which used up a fantastic amount of money, but did not succeed. Pat cried each time she was taken to the hospital, and the mother felt terribly guilty about the whole thing."

Philips had discovered that it was the mother herself who had brought the girl out of the basement.

"She said, 'I had the feeling that she was going down there into a hole, and I couldn't stand it anymore!' But she's still resentful of the fact that the child in the wheelchair is scratching the furniture. I don't know what to do with this woman's conflicting feelings. She feels that all her kids are a drag. She said last week, 'When people ask how Pat is, I feel like throwing up!'

"I see the mother once a week now, and have talked to the counseling center. The social worker there told me that the mother is depressed about not having the energy to go back to school. At the moment, she's upset by their unpainted fence. She says, 'It's an insult to people who come to the house.' I asked who these people are; she says, 'The bridge club.' She's convinced that they are better than she is. She got very angry with me when I asked her what good painting the fence would do. She thought I was making fun of her."

Many of the motifs of the first session were repeated and emphasized in the second. In particular, Philips underlined his impression that everyone connected with the case was becoming exhausted. The husband, he said, "looks *drained* all the time," and worked overtime as often as possible, not primarily to earn more money, but to "get away from his family, and who can blame him?" The handicapped child was racked with guilt about the trouble she caused her mother, and was spending her days listlessly staring at television.

The mother was "just on the edge of being able to control herself and I don't detect much improvement." She was barely able to cling to the shreds of her "suburban façade," though she forced herself to "put on a front to my secretary when she walks out of my office door." She felt that "I'll have this kid for the rest of my life," and that she had to give so much to her child that she had no energy left to use elsewhere. She worked part-time in her father's photographic studio, where she felt exhausted by the necessity of talking to customers.

"She hates herself, she practically says so," Philips continued. "I suspect she's been this way for years, putting up a front, 'I can do anything; I'm confident; I can juggle all the schedules and take care of everything—house, church, social commitments.' And I think the whole thing was phony; and when the crisis came on, everything began to crash."

Throughout Philips' presentation, it appeared that he himself still felt drained and trapped by Jane's disturbance. "She isn't contented. She *won't* be contented. Am *I* supposed to make her feel contented?" he asked in real anguish.

"She wants to be relieved of the burden of her daughter, but she worries whenever the kid is away. She wants to be emotionally strong enough to go back to school, but the life of the whole family was upset by her studying. She wants all her problems solved at once. She wants her husband to take over. She wants *me* to tell her what to do. I just don't know what I can do for her," Philips continued wearily. "Sometimes I think the only thing I do that is genuinely supportive is to pat her shoulder as she goes through my office door. The counseling service wants more cooperation from her so they can help the daughter. She runs from them, but she will come and talk to me. The counseling people think she's pretty sick. They say that she hasn't grieved properly for the death of her mother."

In an aside, Philips remarked that his parishioner had told him that she wanted to do away with herself; and that, after her mother's funeral, she had chosen a burial plot for herself near her sister's grave. When the group attempted to inquire further into these issues, Philips evaded their questions.

The consultee remained caught between contradictory impulses. On the one hand, he felt compelled to shoulder the entire burden of the case, and still insisted that no other sources of help were available to his parishioner. When Jane's father, however, had asked Philips whether he should offer his daughter money to go to a psychiatrist, Philips had told him not to interfere, because he felt that this would wound the pride of the husband. On the other hand, in order to protect himself from being drained by what he considered a lost cause, Philips was pulling away from Jane. He denied the seriousness of her suicide threat; and when the consultant asked him to assess the severity of Jane's depression, he insisted, despite the warnings of the counseling center, "I don't think she's terribly badly off." He was decreasing the frequency of his contacts, now seeing her only once a week. He reported with perplexity that while she had canceled one appointment—which had cheered him—she seemed disturbed when he did not offer her another.

The consultant and the group helped Philips to realize that he was, in fact, giving much support to his parishioner and her daughter despite his despondent thoughts to the contrary. He had, for example, found a job for the girl in the church school, which got her out of the house for a few hours a week, thus raising her spirits and relieving the mother's sense of pressure. Nevertheless, the group urged him to see that the burden of Jane's care was best shared by a number of different people and agencies. The consultant, for example, suggested that the woman might be helped by joining a group of other parents of handicapped youngsters.

"She wouldn't have to be ashamed in front of people who shared the same problem as herself," he explained. "They would accept her contradictory feelings about her child without being shocked by them; and in that group, she wouldn't have to worry about being inferior to the others. It's a big step to join a group like that; but once in, I've known people to stay for years."

"She won't associate with groups for the handicapped," Philips insisted.

"You should encourage her," Waters said. "I always try to

move people out of a one-to-one relationship with me into a wider social context as soon as possible where there are people more competent to deal with the situation."

"Often, you know," the consultant continued, "another mother can do more for someone like that than a doctor or anyone else. Another mother can *feel* the pain; and they are the *real* authorities on the problem of living with a handicapped youngster."

"You may be right," Philips said doubtfully. "But she's caught in this great isolation of suburbia. She doesn't know people like that. She didn't even know there was another kid at Patricia's school in a wheelchair. But you may be right; maybe I should pursue this a little further than I have."

"You realize, I'm sure," said the consultant, "that when you suggest to her that she join this group, she will balk. That's only to be expected. You might ease the way a bit if you could get some information about these groups first, like where and how often they meet, and the names of some of the persons involved. That might take some of the strangeness out of it for her."

Philips was pleased as the idea began to seem more practicable. "I will make some inquiries," he said. "This is something I can offer to her."

"You might also make things easier," Moss suggested, "if you could get someone to take her to the first meeting. I've found that that makes a difference—when they don't have to walk in as strangers."

"The odds are," said the consultant, "that you'll be trying a number of things before one of them works. But I think this is worth a fair amount of effort because I would guess that if she would join, the other women will tell her that they have feelings about their own youngsters, or have had such feelings in the past, that are like what she's going through. And if some of that can be legitimized, she'll have one less heavy weight on her."

These suggestions not only gave Philips a way of getting his parishioner to an effective, outside source of support; they also encouraged him to explore a resource which might prove useful in other cases, by surveying the self-help groups available to parents of handicapped children in his region.

The counseling service had reported that Jane refused to discuss her feelings about her daughter; but Philips had been able to introduce the topic successfully. It may be remembered that the consultant had warned Philips not to explore this area; but the consultee, as was his prerogative, had chosen to ignore this advice, and had apparently been proved right. Throughout this case, despite severe inhibitions, Philips nevertheless continued to act with considerable autonomy, picking and choosing among ideas offered by the group according to how he perceived the needs of the situation.

"Is she worrying about appearances and putting up a front with you, too?" White asked.

"No," Philips admitted with some surprise.

"So she is developing a real trust with you at least." Philips looked somewhat more cheerful.

"Let me get this straight," the consultant said. "Recently, when you said, 'Let's meet next week,' she put it off. Now, I agree, to meet once a week has a natural feel—it's repetitive and you can schedule it. But it may not match her needs. It might be good to listen for what she wants. It might be something less formal than what you are offering. Maybe what you think you are giving is time: but what she's getting is a sense of your concern."

"The demands on me are such," Philips said, "that I'm scared to death that if I don't set an hour with her, I'm not going to give her the time she needs."

"It might not take an hour, though," the consultant said. "Her needs might be such that it won't necessarily take sixty minutes to deliver it."

"True," said Philips.

"She might want to decide that, and not have you decide it," added White.

"Suppose I let her call me when she wants an appointment? But then I'd have to gauge whether she *would* call."

The group agreed emphatically that this was a risky business.

"Let's think about this, and discuss it again," the consultant said, "since *we* have now run out of time."

In considering this session, the consultant felt that many of the points of the previous meeting had been reinforced, and that Philips now seemed somewhat more receptive to the notion of sharing Jane's care with others who might have competence more specialized than his own. A serious problem, however, had now been introduced, the safety of the parishioner. It was clear that Philips feared that the woman was highly disturbed and possibly suicidal. With almost superstitious awe he described the cracking of her "suburban façade" and the draining of energy from Jane and her family. Although there was evidence of exaggeration in Philips' assessment of the case, nevertheless, it was possible that reality and illusion were indeed very close. The evidence supported the assumption that the woman really was in acute difficulties, and in fact might commit suicide. The social worker had said that Jane had not mourned her mother in a healthy way. She was menopausal. She was feeling unworthy and panicky about her own and her family's future. All this tended to make the picture look ominous.

One of the more fascinating and complicating features of this case, and one of the points which posed the greatest challenge to the consultant's technique, was the fact that Philips' fears and the actual circumstances lay so close together. It appeared that Jane did indeed need a psychiatrist, that Philips, alone, was unequal to the situation; and that in the absence of fairly prompt medical intervention, the danger of further deterioration was real. But despite these facts, Philips was reacting inappropriately. Instead of meeting the emergency in an orderly, disciplined way, he was thrown into panic and despondency himself by issues that confused and frightened him.

He felt that it rested on him alone to avert an outcome which he was convinced was inevitable. So he fought on, singlehanded, while at the same time, he tried to safeguard himself from the guilt of failing in the case, by denying that danger existed, by mentioning suicide as though it were not a serious threat. The consultant in reviewing the data, therefore, decided that if Jane's condition did not improve by the next session, he would insist that she be sent for a psychiatric evaluation.

chapter 6

A Successful Case—
Part II: Resolution

The next session found Philips looking more unhappy than
ever, but persistent in his search for help.

"Well fellows," he began, "are you ready for the next exciting chapter of my lady?"

"Give me a one sentence synopsis," said Griffin, who had
missed the previous meeting.

"This lady is depressed," Philips said heavily.

"Oh?" asked Griffin.

"There's been no change. This lady is *still* depressed, I'm not
able to get her undepressed. . . . I'm not sure if God really
cares anymore."

"Is that your thought or hers?" Griffin asked.

The consultant moved at once to divert the discussion from
Philips' feelings, since it was clear not only that he was indeed
depressed, but also that he had built up sufficient trust in, and
reliance on, the group to be ready to expose his emotional
links to the case at the least opportunity. This is one of the
technical difficulties associated with multiple sessions on the
same case. Inevitably, as the deeper issues of the parishioner's
situation are dwelt on, the intimate links of the consultee with
the material rise to the surface; hence, there are greater de-

mands than ever on the consultant to safeguard the minister's privacy.

Once attention had been drawn away from this inadvertently tactless remark, Philips continued: "I now wonder whether I should put her in the category of another lady who contacted me the week after I arrived in my present parish. She was very depressed, and she said to me, 'Have you ever heard of anyone coming out of a depression like mine?' Then, last month, I talked to the chaplain at the local mental hospital. He asked me if I knew this lady from my area who had just been admitted. It was the same one. I said I had seen her a week earlier, when she had again asked me the very same question, 'Have you ever known anyone to come out of a depression like mine?' The chaplain said, 'Is that so? That's what she asked me seven years ago, when she was hospitalized for several months in another mental hospital that I was associated with!' "

The consultant felt that a highly important problem had now emerged. For some reason beyond the purview of consultation, Philips seemed to have particular difficulty with cases of depression, since he evidently shared the second woman's pessimism about its prognosis. When this parishioner had asked her question, Philips had not been able to reassure her; and now, in a thinly disguised manner, he was referring the question to the group. Apparently it was not only Jane's problem that inhibited him, but an entire category of cases which are far from rare in the population. Therefore, if Philips were helped to cope with Jane's depression, he might then use the experience to deal with many other parishioners as well.

"More specifically," Philips continued, "my lady is really no further along, and I'm no further along with her."

Questioning by the group, however, revealed that some progress was discernible, at least in Philips' approach to the family.

"It was very helpful to me when you people suggested that I

see the husband. After the meeting here, I phoned the husband and asked him to come with her for a joint meeting. This will be the first time I'll be sitting down with the two of them together, and I don't really know if this is a step in the right direction or not. He is rather . . . unsure of himself, but a good man. She would like him to be stronger, and yet she dominates him on every occasion when he tries to be strong. I don't know exactly what I'm going to do with whatever we talk about on Monday. Another thing is, her meetings with me are very painful. She gets no quick relief. All I do is bring up painful subjects and we discuss them. She feels no better upon leaving than coming. That's my distinct feeling."

"And she expects to feel better?" Green asked.

"Yes!"

"Why would she still be coming if she gets nothing from it?"

"Because *I* want her to. . . . I feel like I'm getting into a box!"

The consultant shifted the discussion to another topic to lower tension and to explore a key factor in the case.

"How does this lady talk about the future?" he asked.

"She says, 'I don't know what's going to happen to me. I don't know what's going to happen to my children.' "

With this additional reminder that Jane might be contemplating suicide, the consultant prepared to make a major intervention. He wanted to convince Philips to enlarge the range of supports available to his parishioner, and, if possible, to make a serious attempt to get her to see a psychiatrist. In order to do this, the consultant had to break through the minister's defensive denial of danger, to convince him of the realistic threat to Jane's life, while, on the other hand, helping him to accept the equally realistic possibilities of the situation. The consultant wanted Philips to realize that with effective, flexible management not only could a catastrophe be averted, but the depression itself could be cured.

"No matter who does anything," Philips went on, "you lose.

And her husband, he walks with hunched shoulders. He's a beaten man."

"What's the status with the counseling service?" the consultant asked.

"I went to a staff conference on the case," Philips answered, "and we discussed the whole thing and agreed that for the time being, I would substitute for the person working directly with the mother." Jane, it appeared, was becoming more isolated than ever from mental health supervision.

The consultant now prepared to act. He waited, with an eye on the clock, for an opening in the discussion into which he could move. He determined to stress the risk to the parishioner, while keeping, with the help of the group, a cool, matter-of-fact atmosphere that would dampen alarm.

"I don't get the impression," the consultant began, "that this lady is getting enough support. It sounds to me as though she is having a pretty tough time. I winced a bit when you told us that she said, 'I wonder what will become of the children.' When depressed parents talk like that, I lean forward to see what that might mean."

Philips argued hotly.

"Wait a bit," the consultant said, "you said that she was expressing concern about the younger children at that point, not the handicapped youngster?" Philips agreed. "Is there anything wrong with them?" Philips admitted that they were all right. "But if there's no reason to worry about the kids because of something happening in their own lives, there's more reason to assume that she may be talking about herself, which makes me a bit uncomfortable."

"I wonder, though," Philips said, still denying that matters could indeed be so serious. "The younger kids are boys. Perhaps she wants the father to do more for them. Do you think he could be more involved? To give them a stronger father image?"

"Well," said the consultant, "you did tell us that she wanted

her husband to be more dominating; and if he could be helped
to be stronger, it might be very beneficial for the whole family." The consultant was determined to increase Philips' interest in the role of the husband wherever possible.

"This depression might be caused by menopause," White
suggested. "And it might go on and get worse."

"If it is menopause," said the consultant, "that weighs
things even more toward the chance of critical things happening. I think this woman would use a fair amount of her
strength to cover up as long as she could in order to safeguard
her self-image. The fact that she has now come out into the
open with you at least may be a measure of the strain she's
under."

Several members of the group sighed and made despondent
remarks. Philips gradually joined in. This was what the consultant wanted, an acknowledgment of the seriousness of the
woman's plight by the entire group so that Philips would be
supported in accepting the unpalatable fact.

"How much is known of how the husband sees his wife's
problem?" the consultant asked.

"I think he feels completely helpless and a little impatient
with it," Philips said. "He just walks around with this hangdog
expression all the time."

"What I'm really wondering is, does he think things are
worse than they've been?"

"Good question. I haven't really asked him. I see him
around now and again. He's in one of the church clubs. But I
haven't really known how to approach him. He comes to his
club because he's getting away from the family for a bit, so I
really hesitate to get into discussion with him about all the
problems at home. . . . I'm not sure he's *capable* of understanding emotional intricacies."

The consultant wondered how much of Philips' assessment
of the husband's attitude was based on real knowledge, and
how much was a projection onto the other man of the minis-

ter's own sense of futility and desire to escape. The psychiatrist felt that Philips should be brought to recognize the husband as a potential ally in caring for Jane and in relieving the minister's own sense of lonely responsibility.

"Is it your impression that he is worried about her safety?" the consultant asked.

"He stayed home that first morning," Moss said.

Philips seemed shaken. "She won't hear of him staying home usually because they need the money. She must have been feeling *really* bad to let him stay home that first day!"

"Now it seems to me," the consultant continued, "that the first time you described this family, the possibility of a psychiatric evaluation was mentioned."

"She said," Philips answered quickly, " 'I'm not as sick as that, am I?' and there was the lack of money. I didn't recommend it because I didn't see how they would pay for it. I guess there *are* clinics, but I don't know what they are or where they are."

"The family might have assumed that contact with a psychiatrist is necessarily a long-term venture," the consultant said. "They might not, for example, have differentiated treatment from evaluation."

"That's interesting," said Philips after a pause. Apparently he had not considered the point either.

"Perhaps the family counseling service has someone who does the evaluation," Apple suggested.

"Yes, I could ask them," Philips agreed.

"Up till now," the consultant continued, "we haven't established whether there is a psychiatrist in this center at all. I'm thinking of her seeing someone who is thoroughly familiar with psychiatric medication, who would know whether prescribing antidepressants would be a good idea."

"To keep her from killing herself?" asked Philips timidly. Now that an avenue to help was opening, the consultee was able to acknowledge the existence of the risk which he had been trying to evade up till then.

"I am much impressed by this picture of a depressed mother under so much stress talking about her children's future in these particular terms," the consultant explained.

"She's certainly worrying about the future. She says, 'Am I going to feel in the spring, when the next night-school course starts, the way I feel now? Then all the work that I've done up till now will be wiped out.' I keep trying to bring back things to right now, but she always brings us back to this point."

"So here's a lady who's saying in December, 'Am I going to be this depressed in March?' " Waters asked.

"It's exactly what the other woman was saying," Philips said eagerly. " 'Have you ever heard of someone pulling out of a depression like mine?' "

"If she were to seriously think of suicide," Apple said, "how would she go about it? Pills? Slashed wrists?"

Philips looked horrified and shook his head.

"How is she with firearms?" Moss asked. "Are there any around the house?"

"I don't know," Philips admitted, still shaken. Then, after a pause, "She works in her father's photography shop. She might swallow developing chemicals."

"I think," said Griffin in a decided tone, "that would make her horribly sick, but I doubt it would kill her."

"People generally signal before they harm themselves," Moss added. Everyone murmured agreement.

"This whole case really intrigues me," said the consultant, catching the group's attention, "because it sounds so similar to what happened recently to one of my kid brother's closest friends. They are both working for Ph.D.'s in economics, and this fellow was scheduled to take his orals. Twice he froze at the last minute and couldn't go through with them. The second time, when he canceled a day before the exam, he phoned my brother in a panic and said, 'Get me to a psychiatrist! I can't go on! I'll never get my Ph.D.!' So my brother called me, and we fixed him up with a colleague of mine; and every now and then, this young man would phone up and say, 'I can't go on with this!' My brother would answer, 'Nonsense, of course you can do it. You're perfectly competent,' which I then told him was the classic mistake, since the answer always came back, 'I'm not! I never carry things through!' So my brother decided that the answer for this particular boy was, 'Then it's time you did!'

"About a month before his orals were scheduled for the third time, he said to my brother, 'You know, it's a funny thing. Nothing much has changed in the last three months, but I don't feel the same way I did before. I've got the orals coming up; nothing's changed; and yet, I know I'm going to take them.' A week ago yesterday, he took them and passed. Toward the end, the depression manifested itself as a terrifically bad temper. He bit my brother's head off a few days before the exam; but he pulled through."

"He was able to take the anger and direct it out, not inward at himself," mused Philips.

"Was he having continued psychiatric help?"

"Yes," said the consultant. "He was depressed and he felt inadequate. He, I suspect, like your parishioner, had the unfortunate habit of putting very high stakes on everything he did. His whole identity rested on every single throw of the dice, until all the A's in his courses didn't count any more, but the B + 's were a tragedy. One of the things he had to learn was to have mercy on himself. But the point was that he felt, especially the second time he panicked so badly, that he would never, ever be able to face that exam and that would be the end of his career. A few months later, he just took his orals."

"Without the external factors changing?" asked Philips.

"Nothing changed, except that he was now getting a lot of support to tide him over a difficult period. There was the psychiatrist; and all the people around him were ready to help. His girl friend was very firm with him, and said, 'Cut it out! You are brilliant but you can't accept that, so sit down and work!' She was very intelligent about this, and actually gave him assignments. He said, 'I can't pick up a book. I can't study. My mind goes blank at the sight of a book.' She said, 'I don't care. You sit in front of that book and turn the pages.' "

"They're still together?" Moss asked.

"They just got engaged. One's first impulse with such a person is to be terribly gentle and to go along with his gambits. But here, a good shove from people who obviously cared really worked."

"Yes," said Philips briskly, "I do think the attitude of my parishioner's husband is the worst possible thing for her. That's one reason I want to work with him at once, to see if he can be more supportive. At the moment, when she says, 'I feel terrible,' he says, 'Yes, I know, dear.' "

The consultee's manner had now become energetic and less anxious as he came to realize that Jane's depression might improve. Philips had found proof of her inevitable deterioration in the case of the second depressed parishioner who had never recovered despite years of treatment. The consultant opposed this gloomy view not by direct, cognitive arguments, but by offering the counterweight of another case, where the outcome had been quite different. By answering Philips' fears in the terms that he had chosen, the consultant achieved faster results.

"Maybe the husband would do more if he could see some clear-cut alternative," the consultant continued. "Maybe he's doing so little because he doesn't see what he *might* do."

"I think I'd better take all this advice down," said Philips suddenly, pulling out pen and notebook and making notes hurriedly.

"This man has been in this situation quite a while," the consultant added. "He might have a pretty restricted view of what the situation is really like."

"You're absolutely right," said Philips. "Especially since there is such a hopeless tone about so much of what she says. I'll try and get this solved by next time so I don't have to bring this up again," he added in some embarrassment.

"I'd like to hear what happens," said the consultant firmly, and the group agreed. "I'd like to know what the husband's views are of the whole situation. And one shouldn't discount a psychiatric evaluation. Treatment was a great help to my brother's friend and it might work here too. I think you mentioned at one point that Jane's father was willing to pay for her to see someone?"

"But would she be willing to go?" asked White.

"It seems to me," the consultant said, "that she might wonder whether psychiatric evaluation might imply that she had to give up her contacts with her minister. She might think that this was a substitution, a replacement, while it need only be the *addition* of another point of view." Implicitly, this was reassurance for Philips that he would not be shouldered out of the case, since he so clearly wanted to remain the primary caregiver.

"Well," said Apple, "it's hard to predict people's reactions to suggestions like this. For all we know, she might welcome it as a great relief. Perhaps if you raised the question with her, you'd get an answer."

"Yes," Philips agreed uncertainly.

"Does the husband think of this possibility?" the consultant asked.

"I don't know," Philips admitted.

"He sounds like someone who keeps his shoulder to the wheel and doesn't look up as often as he might."

"I think I could help him," said Philips, "by asking him what he'd like to see, what possibilities he sees for this entire situation. I think I could really listen to what he has to say."

"You'd have to be very careful," White advised, "when you brought up the possibility of a psychiatrist that Jane didn't get the idea that you wanted to get rid of her."

The group agreed.

"You'd have to define things," the consultant said. "An evaluation doesn't presuppose an outcome of long-term treatment."

"Perhaps you could find a psychiatrist who could explain this to her with whom you could discuss the matter afterward," Griffin suggested.

"Man, I'd like to know that psychiatrist," Philips remarked. The group then spent a quarter of an hour exploring the various possible sources of psychiatric care in Philips' area and in suggesting ways of contacting them.

As the session ended, the consultant said, "After all, Jane is suffering from a depression. That is not some vague discomfort of the spirit. It's a medical condition, a real disease, and doctors have ways of treating it. Why should this woman suffer so much when she might be helped?"

Philips looked immeasurably relieved to have the condition that he had been regarding fearfully reduced to a relatively comprehensible medical category.

One might legitimately ask why the consultant had spent so much time urging Philips to get his parishioner to a psychiatrist instead of simply offering to see Jane himself. Had he done so, he would have disrupted the consultation relationship by becoming an active agent, relieving the minister of a measure of direct responsibility for his case, and hence depriving him of the opportunity to expand his own skills. It would also have been subtly belittling, since it would have confirmed for a man who was already unsure of his competence in a particular category of cases that he was indeed beyond his depth, and that the consultant was now coming in to rescue the situation. This loss of self-esteem would not occur if the consultee were himself to decide that mental health care was indicated for a parishioner after weighing the ideas of the group. He would then retain his autonomy and self-respect.

By not offering to intervene, the consultant was ensuring that his own role in the minister's work would be temporary. Consultation, after all, is designed to be time-limited. Direct intervention in the case would imply that in future the minister could again refer people to the consultant. The latter would then become an indispensable, continuing part of the clergyman's network of resources.

In consultation, the case at issue is used as a pattern for similar ones in the future so that the minister will learn to manage an ever greater proportion of such situations on his own; but this increased self-reliance means that he must also learn to identify specialized needs in certain parishioners which do require referral elsewhere. Therefore, one of the goals of the consultant is to teach the consultee the importance and the method of establishing and maintaining links with a range of resources in his own community. This end would hardly be served if the consultant were simply to give the clergyman an easy alternative to forming such contacts by himself entering into competition with local specialists. That might seem cheaper in the short run, though it would turn the consultant into a traditional clinician, whose professional activities were perforce limited to his own case load, which, however it grew, could never satisfy the needs of all the mentally ill in the community. But in the long run, it would be self-defeating, since it would leave the minister stranded if he or the consultant were ever to move from that area. The clergyman would then be no better equipped than before to find another psychiatrist to whom he could refer. Consequently, this consultant pressed Philips on a number of occasions to discover and use various facilities in this community rather than to muddle through on his own or to rely on the consultant. And it is significant that Philips, as an experienced consultee, never asked the psychiatrist to see Jane, since he knew that this was inappropriate.

Having said this, we must add a proviso. In cases where there is a clear and immediate danger to the parishioner, such as risk of suicide, the consultant, by virtue of his psychiatric training and the fact that he is a clinician licensed by the community, does have responsibility if there should be a catastrophe. He must use his judgment, therefore, to assess, albeit on the basis of hearsay evidence, how acute and imminent the danger might be. If he decides that it is too great, he may have to push the consultee aside and step into the case in order to protect the parishioner's life or sanity.

The consultee, having told the consultant of a possible risk, can rely on the fact that the latter will bear basic professional responsibility for the outcome, even though the consultee might have ignored advice from the specialist which could have averted tragedy. In practice, consultants are rarely forced to intervene in this way, since professionals of the level of sophistication to become consultees in the first place by and large know when the danger level is rising. Then, rather than asking for consultation, they refer the case at once to local hospitals or agencies. Nevertheless, the possibility of such a situation occurring has to be borne in mind.

In this case, the psychiatrist judged that the risk of Jane attempting suicide was high, but not high enough that he need personally intervene. He knew that she was being watched by her father and husband, and by a family doctor who was currently treating her for a chronic respiratory condition. He could also rely on Philips who, despite his perplexity, was completely adequate to any real crisis. At the moment, the minister was inhibited by his own emotional links to the abstract issues of the case; but his view of Jane's plight was clear enough for the consultant to have no doubt that if real and immediate danger threatened, Philips would act appropriately. What the consultant wanted to ensure was that matters need never approach so near a crisis—that Jane would be helped long before she was driven to desperation.

Philips left the meeting in an energetic and hopeful mood. The following week, he still looked cheerful and relaxed.

"Well?" everyone asked.

"I saw them both the other night. I think one of the most helpful ideas that came out of last week was that the husband had to be helped to get some clear notions of how he might handle the situation. So we all met, and it was very, very good. She was more animated—she actually yelled a few times, which was fine, since every other time I'd seen her, she'd whispered. This time she was much more relaxed.

"I brought up the whole question of how her depression affected Patricia and her husband—how they felt about it, and how she felt about it herself. It was very constructive, and helpful. He relaxed, because I was able to challenge her position, as he had not been able to do, while at the same time supporting her but not always going along with her. I intend to see them together again."

"What did the husband feel that this had done for him?" the consultant asked.

"I think he felt relaxed from the burden of taking care of Jane's problem all by himself. I think he felt ever so much better that I was there with him and Jane. I can't put my finger on it more clearly. I think he expressed his confusion about her; I don't know if he'd done so before."

"And their interaction was about as you'd understood?" the consultant asked.

"It was better than I thought. Somehow, I felt that both of them were more open to each other than I'd expected. And she was so much more relaxed. It could be she was discovering things."

"What one might hope for," the consultant said, "is that with your backing, he might feel stronger and be more supportive to her, while his own anxiety about the situation is reduced. That would be an ideal combination; and at this point, it doesn't look impossible."

"My impression was that he was just beginning to get a glimmer that there might be some possibility of improvement," Philips continued to recall. "I think that over the years, he'd sort of turned off, and had hidden from the fact of her emotional upset. I thought that he was now beginning to be willing to look again."

"He might feel that he could afford to notice more, if he feels less alone," the consultant said.

"That's a good way to put it," Philips agreed. "I think this was what was beginning to happen to him. He made some self-deprecating remarks about his work, and I didn't accept them. I just felt that I could infuse a little more confidence in him about himself. The first time I talked to him alone, the more he talked, the more depressed he became, and I just terminated—I didn't know what to do with it. He didn't understand her, he didn't understand himself. This time, there wasn't any of that, he was less hopeless."

"I wonder if a couple of months from now," the consultant said, "it will turn out that the fact that you and the husband established contact with each other has helped both of you to support her; that it will produce greater results than would have come if each of you had worked separately."

"I had been completely unaware until this session that he had the feeling that he had to bear this thing all by himself, and he just didn't know what to do with this woman," Philips went on. "Now he has found somebody else who understands the situation and who was giving some alternatives to just sinking into the morass of misery that he saw himself falling into. There are enough strengths in him that there can be a change; and I have the feeling that she wants him to be stronger. Because although she basically runs everything, she'd prefer it if he ran things."

"I think you're telling us more than that," Waters said. "I think you're answering the question you quoted last week: can a depressed woman get better? It seems that you're now saying, there *are* possibilities here."

"That's true," said Philips quietly.

Here was evidence of success. Philips was now talking of Jane's and her husband's future and of his own work with the family in a hopeful, energetic tone. He no longer saw himself carrying the weight of the case alone, since he had discovered that the husband could be helped to assume part of the burden. Philips was no longer so ambivalent about Jane; he could accept her domineering manner with more tolerance and detachment.

Half an hour later, an even more hopeful sign appeared. After a review of the progress of a case presented by another member of the group some weeks earlier, Philips interrupted: "Can I ask a question about a depressed person? I referred last time to a woman who asked me, 'Does a depression like mine ever get better?' She called me again last night and she sounded better than I've ever heard her before; but she said, 'I've got such an awful depression and I don't think it will ever go away. They did shock treatment on me and it didn't work.' At this point in the past I had listened. Last night I didn't listen, I talked—and I wouldn't let her continue her story. Would you say this was a good way to deal with a person like this? Her husband was going away for three weeks and she wanted someone to be with her at suppertime, which is the toughest part of the day for her. I said I'd try to find someone in the congregation to come and visit her at that time. I think this came to me because of your story about your brother's friend, when your brother didn't go along with him when he said, 'Oh, I can't take that exam.' And your brother said, 'Yes, you *can* do it;' and that was a way of approaching the whole situation."

Here was a noticeable reversal of Philips' earlier attitude and manner. When he heard again from his chronically depressed parishioner whose plight had so upset him the week before, he no longer reacted with undue sensitivity. When he felt that "she sounded much better than I've ever heard her before," he was hearing her through his own greater self-confidence. *She* had not changed, *he* had. Instead of responding to her stereotyped gambit, in which she made a bid for his sympathy, he tried to soothe her, and they both felt hopeless, he now interrupted the sterile pattern with an offer of real help. The woman was suffering in the absence of her husband. The minister could send her company to tide her over the worst period of her day. Instead of entering into collusion with her to confirm her in her identity as a case of hopeless depression, therefore, he acted positively to reduce her suffering.

What fascinated the consultant was the disappearance of inhibition from Philips' manner—of the stiff, literal grasping after any concrete suggestion from the group to rescue him from confusion. On this occasion, the consultee had assimilated a new point of view so well that he was able to use it selectively and to abstract from it in order to apply its principle to a quite different situation. He was thus acting once again like a fully independent, mature professional whose confidence and initiative were renewed.

It was clear that this process could not have taken place in one or two sessions. It required at least four meetings for Philips to work through his deep perplexity. What may seem surprising at first is that the group did not resent so much time and attention being given to one case. On the contrary, there was active participation throughout in helping the consultee to explore the material and in considering the implications of the issues raised for their own work. As the entire group came to share Philips' concern for Jane, so they participated in his relief and renewal of energy when they succeeded in helping him to find a way out.

chapter 7

The Versatility of a
Consultation Group

The previous chapters may have given the erroneous impression that consultation is a rigidly cerebral process, which shies away from the feelings of participants. In practice, in the course of case discussions, such groups often give direct advice and sympathy to troubled consultees, although the consultant must always guard against unwarranted prying into private feelings while ensuring that the group's efforts are ultimately used to bolster and expand the consultee's mastery of his role. This may be illustrated by the following case, which shows the range of functions that such a group can carry out if it is used flexibly.

Two weeks before this session, a curate, Henry Gosling, had agreed to present a case. When the group assembled, however, Gosling said that his presentation had been driven out of his head by news broken to him the night before. He had learned that his church was discharging him because the congregation could no longer afford his salary.

"I'm not asking for sympathy," he said, "but I just don't know what to do. I know this is a national problem. I'm in effect on the job market, a reasonably tight job market, as I understand. This has done a lot of things to me psychologically. I'm just out of seminary; I was just getting on my feet;

and I find myself in a position I never thought I'd be in as a clergyman—which was pretty naïve of me—that is, the position of being expendable. I realize that people don't want my services anymore. I guess there are reasons for that. It costs the parish about $10,000 to support a clergyman, and things are tight. And then the second thing is the disappointment. I'd just built up some good pastoral relationships with people. They weren't perhaps as deep as I'd have liked, but I'm known to people, and I'm getting some feedback. I got a note from a woman the other day saying that the sermon I'd preached the week before was one of the best she'd heard in a long time. That really made me feel good. I've got good enough relations with one layman in the parish so that he told me off one time; and I'd rather have that than polite indifference. I thought that if he felt free enough to do that, some good things must have been going on. I've been trying to start a draft-information center; and I've been working with some runaway teenagers in town. I don't want to sound egoistical about it, but I have been a prime mover in getting people off their butts in this community and getting things started.

"I'm not sure what I should be doing now. That's the thing. I have certain responsibilities to that parish, certain ones to myself, certain ones to the church, and yet I feel that some of it's been cut off, if you know what I mean. I just don't know what to do."

The consultant and the group realized the complexity of this appeal. The young man was clearly distraught and was asking for help in mastering a personal crisis, which, in this early stage, had left him feeling rejected, disillusioned, and lost. He thus needed an infusion of emotional support to ensure that this upheaval would be a stimulus to growth, not a blow that might lower his mental resilience in the future. On another level, the curate was asking for guidance at a turning point in his professional life. He needed help, therefore, in facing the practical aspect of his predicament, and assistance in gaining sufficient perspective to see this hitherto incomprehensible event in rational terms of organizational and community dynamics, understanding of which might ease his career in his next parish.

At this stage of the session, the group reacted to the curate's distress with great tact. Since the young man was close to tears, the consultant pulled down the emotional level by starting a general discussion about actual conditions in the church —about the state of the job market for clergy and about the way parishes are financed. The group joined in giving a lugubrious account of the narrowing of national and local church resources and of the consequent precariousness of ministers' jobs and of basic church programs. One of the men noted that a new ruling of the diocese, which established minimum salaries for clergy, was a mixed blessing.

"It seems to me, that they should have consulted the rectors and the vestries before they passed that ruling. It's all very well to say that wealthy parishes ought to pay higher salaries but it hits the poorer ones very hard—they have to meet the minimum, too. Now that there is a recession, it makes it harder than ever. It's just all wrong! It interferes with the relations between a minister and his congregation. I know of a number of churches that can't afford curates anymore."

"You know," sighed White, "there are a lot of clergy out of work now. In my younger days it was inconceivable to find a minister without a parish. I couldn't *imagine* a clergyman out of work—unless he was ill or something. It was the bishop's responsibility to see that you had a job. Nowadays, some men become teachers, or social workers, or something, but what about us older men? We don't have any marketable skills."

"Well," said Green, "I think something will have to be done before long; something will come out of church convention this year, because there isn't even enough money budgeted to bring salaries in subsidized parishes up to the minimum. How can we get the money? The churches aren't paying their quotas to headquarters, so how can the diocese function? The diocese can't afford to pay the clergy and the churches themselves can't or won't pay the clergy, so where do we go? The local parishes aren't living up to their responsibilities either way; and to economize on curates as a way out is nonsensical!"

As the discussion continued, technical financial data were pooled by those with direct access to the deliberations of the Diocesan Council, to various committees of the Annual Convention, and to conditions in other areas. Some mistaken notions about current regulations were corrected; resolutions to support each other in proposals to the convention were made; and dissatisfactions with the present system were aired with grim satisfaction. The morale of the group was now curiously high. Depressing matters had become exciting in congenial company.

Meanwhile, Gosling's dejection was lifting, and he was beginning to add points to the discussion. From being a cast-off waif, he had now been raised into an epitome of the dilemma that his elders were lamenting. His fate had become symbolic of the general malaise in his profession, so that far from being regarded as a failed clergyman, he was now, by implication, a minor martyr, and his views of his own situation were treated by his colleagues as communiqués from the front lines.

Had the group tried to soothe Gosling's feelings directly, by assuring him that he was not a failure, that he had a bright future despite this setback, and by encouraging him to speak of his hopes and disillusionment, they would have weakened him further. Despite the sympathy, he might have broken down and sunk further into self-pity and subsequent embarrassment. As it was, his self-respect was bolstered by the tactful way in which the group treated him. There was no suggestion that he might feel threatened and weak. He was addressed instead as a resilient adult, a colleague in awkward professional straits from whom realistic, mature views could be expected, and whose few self-revealing remarks were heard, but were never openly acknowledged. Furthermore, a more direct ministering to Gosling's feelings would have been of little benefit to the other members of the group, however it might have affected the curate. It is unlikely that they would have derived as much knowledge and comfort from that as they gained from discussing how to combat the conditions which threatened their own professional survival as well as Gosling's.

As the curate's level of tension dropped, he was able to talk of the forces which he identified as determining his predicament.

"Now I don't want to be judgmental, but I think a lot of this is due to lousy planning on the part of vestries. Some of them do really silly things. Take mine, for example. They actually did a whole lot of landscaping that they didn't need, and then they complain that they don't have enough money. It's not that I'm so upset about losing this job. I knew when I came that I'd only stay there for a short time anyway. It's just that I needed the time there to start getting on my feet. And I worked so hard. But the way the vestry behaved was really bad. I'd like to hear what some of you fellows have to say about other vestries."

A number of men agreed that financial planning in many parishes was wretched. Gosling, picking up courage, enlarged his attack to include diocesan administration.

"Those guys should have been sacked as soon as people saw what they were up to! They ran one of the most fiscally irresponsible organizations I've seen in my life! They got unacceptable, *unacceptable* returns on the money they were supposed to invest. They just won't go into capital for salaries, but they will for fancy carvings and a lot of other nonsense they don't need. And the vestries are just as bad. My experience is that when a businessman joins a vestry he forgets all his business sense. He behaves like a blithering fool. It may be okay; it may not; but now my job is on the line!"

A few sympathetic murmurs were heard.

"Well, now that I've let that little salvo go," Gosling continued with a touch of embarrassment——

"You didn't hear anyone disagreeing with you," a colleague interposed quietly.

Indeed, the group was getting obvious vicarious satisfaction from Gosling's outburst; but this remark, which directly responded to one of the curate's self-deprecating comments, made the young man highly uncomfortable, since it showed that someone had noticed his weakness. Although his allusions to his own feelings were indeed bids for pity and reassurance, Gosling was also using them to master what he appeared to see as unworthy thoughts, thoughts in which he consequently did not want to be reinforced.

The consultant quickly diverted the discussion to less personal areas.

"Now, *do* they put that capital in savings banks instead of stocks and funds in this state?" A further discussion ensued about financial management, while Gosling's poise gradually returned.

"Ah, yes," Green sighed, "vestries are very conservative."

"They aren't conservative," Gosling said bluntly, "they are plain stupid. They are really doing a shit job! Those smart bankers are ruining this diocese, they really are. You ought to get some Jewish bankers, then maybe things will improve a bit!"

The group absorbed these outbursts quietly. They allowed Gosling to work off his fury by making provocative, adolescent remarks in front of his elders, without contradicting him. Instead, they supported what they saw as the legitimate facets of his grievance, by echoing those complaints in a restrained key, and linking them to larger impersonal issues of church and community organization. They never allowed the young curate to isolate himself in his complaints, or to grow too extreme in his language. They repeatedly interjected the sense that they, as a collectivity, were confronting similar problems all of which had understandable, though regrettable, causes.

Gradually, the group contained Gosling's fury within reasonable bounds, and then began to move him toward realistic planning for the future.

"Personally," Moss said, "I think you should go and talk to some of the bishop's staff about all of this. I think you could use this as an opportunity to look around."

"Oh, I know what will happen," Gosling said, "I'll go down to see the bishop, and he'll listen to me and then say, 'Gee, that's too bad. I'm sorry, I can't really help you.' That's basically what he'll say."

"Now wait a minute," Griffin said sharply, "that's not what he said the other day to someone whose case was similar to yours. He said to him, 'Remember, whatever happens, you're from this diocese, and we will take care of our own first.' And as a matter of fact, he found him a job."

"Well, that's nice to know. But he doesn't *have* to take care of me," said Gosling hotly. "I don't go for this paternalism. Personally, I have a number of options, because I'm willing to move about the country. I'd just like to find some work, I don't care where it is. Part of my frustration now is, just as I'm beginning, I'm being snatched away."

"Where had you thought of looking for another job?" White asked. Gosling mentioned two states.

"Oh, I'd be careful about that one," Green said. "I'd avoid it, if I were you. That diocese is in a shambles. But I heard the other day that there are some positions available the next state over. It's rural, so I guess it isn't a very popular place to work, but it's beautiful there. So if you don't mind the isolation, you might make some inquiries."

Gosling flew into another rage about the haphazard way in which men had to search for jobs in the church. "There should be a rational way of finding places, not a grapevine!" The men agreed, and quietly suggested possibly useful contacts. Gosling subsided.

By now, the consultant judged Gosling's emotional control to have been sufficiently restored for the young man to be ready to examine the situation with his parish. With the help of the group, therefore, the consultant prodded Gosling into assessing his situation in light of the evidence, rather than allowing his emotions to determine his perceptions, and hence his reactions.

"Let me get this straight," the consultant said. "They are terminating you six months short of the period of your contract?"

"Right."

"And they did this without your having any knowledge of the situation in advance? Don't the rector and the vestry have any say in this?"

"Yes, I'm sorry I didn't make this clear. What usually happens is that when the budget committee presents a budget, the vestry usually passes it. But the vestry has to approve it."

"But the vestry hasn't ruled that as of September 1, you are out?" Apple asked.

"No, but when a congressional committee in the federal government votes thirteen to nothing for something, the bill usually gets through. It's that kind of situation."

"Was it really that overwhelming a vote?" asked a quiet voice.

"What?" said Gosling in surprise.

"In the budget committee—do you know how they voted?"

A long pause. "No."

"Do you know how many there are on the budget committee?"

"I think there are about half a dozen."

"Wouldn't they be outvoted by the rest of the vestry, if the others didn't agree?"

"Well . . ." Gosling was startled by the idea. "But you see, it couldn't happen. If they really wanted to keep me, they'd have to finance a deficit budget. No parish is going to do that, unless they think it's an absolute necessity to have a second man."

"I haven't yet heard evidence that a range of possible solutions were considered for dealing with this financial situation," said the consultant.

"I'm not sure what was considered," Gosling said. "I've got to go back and find that out. I'll have to ask the rector."

"I would wonder, you see, what were the priorities of that budget committee? I presume it's a line-item budget—so much for electricity, so much for tuning the organ, so much for the upkeep of the grounds. So, if they decided that they were spending five thousand dollars too much, did they trim a little here and there, or did they look for the items that came closest to that figure, like the curate's salary? And did they just cut that and feel they'd solved the problem?"

"You're right on the nose," said Waters grimly. Everyone nodded in agreement.

"Yes," said Apple, "I knew a parish that actually cut the rector out. They wanted to pay off their mortgage, and their old rector had retired. The sum closest to the mortgage in the budget was the rector's salary. So they proposed that instead of replacing the rector, they bring in a guest preacher on Sunday for thirty dollars a time, and leave the place locked the rest of the week."

"So," said the consultant to Gosling, "this approach to a budget might be something which one should look at to understand the situation. I'm wondering if there might be other aspects. Might some of the vestrymen be dissatisfied, realistically or unrealistically, with something, and might this be one way of registering that dissatisfaction? Could this tell us anything?"

"I would say that's a strong possibility," said Waters. "I've known parishes that attacked a rector by trying to cut his favorite projects."

"I know a parish," Philips added, "where they didn't fire the rector, they just lowered his salary to five dollars a month, literally."

"So they used the budget as a tool," the consultant said. The ministers agreed.

Here the rest of the clergymen, who were emotionally detached from Gosling's predicament, acted as a medium between him and the consultant. The consultant was offering a range of suggestions on how the behavior of the budget committee might be assessed. In doing so, he would expect to encounter resistance from Gosling, who was still bound by a more simplistic view of the committee's actions: that they were fiscally irresponsible and had consequently run out of money, and were therefore rejecting his contributions to the church rather than economizing in a less vital area. The group, however, served to legitimatize and confirm the more complex ideas that the consultant was proposing. They were saying, in effect, "However far-fetched that might sound in your case, our experience tells us that it is indeed a commonly occurring phenomenon in other parishes." They thereby gave the curate time to hear and assimilate unexpected notions. At this point in the session, however, Gosling made no response, and even appeared oblivious to what was passing. Half an hour later, however, he himself alluded to these ideas in a confident tone as possible motives of the budget committee, as though he had gradually digested these suggestions in the interval and had now accepted them as part of his own understanding of the behavior of his parish.

At the present moment in the discussion, however, this "digestive process" was working over a point made earlier.

"You know," said Gosling suddenly, "I don't really know who's on my budget committee. I know a couple of people, but that's all."

"It must be a very quiet committee," Apple said.

"Yes, a *very* quiet committee," Gosling agreed.

"Does a committee member have to belong to the vestry?" the consultant asked.

"No, they don't," Gosling said. "I think there's a former vestryman, a current one, and the rest I'm not even sure about. That's an obvious thing I should do—find out who's on this committee."

"You might also find out what sorts of experience and interests they have," Waters suggested. "Are they people with human-service concerns, or are they more interested in straight financial and property management?"

"Good idea," said Gosling cheerfully. Terms were now being offered to understand this hitherto mysterious, awesomely powerful committee. Its members did not have to be regarded as anonymous adversaries with limitless influence over the curate's fate who acted from inscrutable motives. Their reasons and prejudices could be discovered, and perhaps countered if they were once identified and opposed rationally. Here the consultant and the group were providing Gosling with both emotional and cognitive support. They were helping him to see that he was not a powerless victim of dark forces. They were also teaching him some lessons on how to operate within a complex social and administrative institution like a parish, where special-interest groups and behind-the-scenes manipulations must be expected, and must be taken into account in any negotiations.

"Do you have a written contract?" Moss asked.

"Yes, I do."

"Bring that to the vestry meeting."

"Can they fire you legally if you've got a contract?"

"Just a minute," cautioned White. "If the contract is with the rector, and the vestry doesn't have any money, I don't see where a contract will help you."

"If they really don't have the money, and the vestry votes

me out, then my agreement with the rector isn't really worth that much, and I could accept that."

"It would be an unhappy victory if you were to force them to keep you, and they didn't want you to stay on," White continued.

"You mean, for the parish?" Philips asked.

"No, I mean for him. It would be most uncomfortable. It's not a situation he would want." Group members argued this for a few minutes back and forth, while Gosling, detached, listened to several alternate ways in which he and the parish might be expected to react in such an eventuality. It was reminiscent of a device of morality plays, in which personifications of a man's opposing urges debate his future intentions more cogently than he himself could; and the man, having listened in silence, can then choose between them.

"I think," Gosling interrupted, suddenly and incoherently, "I should bring up at the vestry meeting the whole question of the clergy providing service. And raise the issue, as dispassionately as I can, what my impression has been, and I may be wrong about this, but I don't think the issue revolves round my personality. On the contrary, I think people have appreciated my being here, with some exceptions, of course. But the issue is, I wonder whether they *have* explored other avenues in the budget, including selling some capital assets. I think that's a legitimate issue to raise."

"Yes," said Griffin carefully. "Now I wonder, would it be most politic for *you* to raise this, or should you ask the rector?"

"I could ask him to do it," said Gosling quickly.

"Yes, because after all, the curate is his responsibility. He had to hire the curate and then get the vestry to pay his salary—which they agreed to do. The fact that the budget people now say that they don't have any more money doesn't absolve either them or the rector of their original responsibility. All of this is really a problem for the rector—an issue of how much he can rely on anything the vestry says."

"That's right. I think that's put extremely well and extremely succinctly," said Gosling, sounding surprised and enlightened.

"Further, you see, politics enters into this. If *you* bring this up, people will think of it as your personal complaint; but if the rector were to speak to it, the underlying issues would have more chance of being aired."

"Yes," said Gosling promptly. "I obviously have a personal stake in this; but I'd like them to understand, for the sake of men who come in the future, that they are playing fast and loose by not having and honoring proper contractual agreements. They're saying, 'We'll take people when times are good, but we'll drop them when things are bad.'"

"They're also saying," a younger minister added, "that they expect to get experienced rectors, but they're not willing to do their share in training men for the ministry. If everyone had that attitude, there would never be any experienced men. Someone might point out to them that they have a responsibility to the whole church, which they aren't living up to."

"Now these might be useful points for you to put to the bishop," Griffin added.

"I think you're both absolutely right," said Gosling. "I think that I should discuss this matter. I am a little hurt by this, frankly." There was a general murmur of "Yes, quite understandable." "But," continued Gosling, "if you go around in a situation like this trying to find a son-of-a-bitch every place, it doesn't do you much good. But the issue is, what kind of responsibilities do they have to guys who come there right out of training?"

This was a revealing interchange, demonstrating how far Gosling's poise had been restored since the beginning of the session. Not only was he now taking a more sophisticated and detached view of the budget committee's actions, but his emotional equilibrium was steadied. This latest allusion to his own sense of hurt was made calmly, as a fact which obviously colored, but had no need to constrain, his attitudes. It was no longer a naked appeal to pity; it was a mature, self-confident acknowledgment of the realities of human responses. The group sensed this renewed strength and, for the first time, openly reacted. Gosling displayed no embarrassment at this, because he felt that his colleagues were not underlining his weakness, but were supporting a factual observation.

"You said you didn't think this was any form of reprisal against you?" the consultant asked, taking advantage of this renewed control.

"I don't feel paranoid about it in that sense," said Gosling calmly. "I just had a friend, a curate in another diocese, and he got into a rip-roaring Donnybrook with his vestry. They put all kinds of pressure on him and on the rector to fire him— and he did. And my friend is literally out selling gasoline now. But that's not my case. But what gets me is that I did such a good job, really I did. I gave some good sermons on the usual bullshit—flag and country stuff. I do have some antiwar posters around the office, and a couple of people did blink when they came in, but nobody said anything."

"As I hear it," the consultant said, "the budget seems to be a way of controlling the parish."

"Right on!" said Gosling.

"So," continued the consultant, "if someone is dissatisfied with something, the first thing they do is withdraw financial support."

"You mean," said Waters, "that emotional stuff is put on a supposedly rational basis?"

"That's just what I was wondering," the consultant answered.

"It's certainly true in the case of individuals," sighed Moss. "Lots of people canceled pledges because of the South Bend

Conference's proposal to grant amnesty to the kids who went to Sweden to escape the draft. I had a lady who threatened to cancel because she found out that I had registered as a Democrat for a primary in which one of our vestrymen was running for selectman."

Gosling looked defiant.

"By the way," asked the consultant, "how negotiable is the budget? Does the budget committee have final say, or can they and the vestry be bargained with?"

"It may be negotiable," Gosling said, "that's what's been brought out today in my case. It gives me a lot of food for thought. I'm going to raise this seriously with the rector like this: granted that things are tight, granted that a lot of things are down, but do we want to truncate our ministry as a way of cutting back in this way?"

"You might make it less drastic than that," Waters cautioned. "You might say, what we are really talking about is six months here; perhaps that bit of the salary can be covered. I mean, this whole financial thing is manipulation, a financial club."

"One of the problems with communication," Gosling said, "is that curates can't even go to a vestry meeting."

"That may be," said the consultant. "But if you can make a good case to the rector, you don't have to go to vestry meetings."

"You may be right," Gosling answered.

"What if the vestry reverses itself?" Apple asked.

"Oh, they might, they might," said Gosling.

"Would you stay on?"

"I'd have to think about that. I might stay on. But you see, what they'd really like me to do, and I'll probably do it, is get a job now, and leave as soon as possible."

"You might give this a bit of thought," his colleague continued, "just in case the whole thing blows over. I grant you it's unlikely, but it's well to be prepared."

Here, once again, a senior clergyman was helping the curate to plan rationally for a variety of possible outcomes to his predicament.

"Look," Gosling said as the session ended, "I want to thank you. I don't want to get emotional about this, but it's been a real help. I mean, when I walked in here I didn't have any idea what I would do. I just couldn't think."

The group broke up in high spirits. "Who wants to present a case next week?" the consultant asked.

"Remember," one of the men added, "if you don't have a problem now, you *will* have by then!"

In this session, the consultant and the group accomplished four tasks. First, they supported Gosling at a time of crisis, when he needed reassurance about his worth as a person and as a clergyman. By treating the curate with warmth and respect, these older, admired colleagues lightened the curate's sense of failure and isolation by the implications of their actions. They consistently treated him as an adult when he was feeling like a frightened child. Had the group made explicit reference to Gosling's obvious upset in the early stages of the session, they might have reinforced his hopelessness by undermining his efforts, obvious at the earliest stages of his presentation, to behave like a man in the face of a catastrophe. It is instructive that Gosling recoiled with embarrassment when a minister responded to one of his self-deprecatory remarks; for while this remark was indeed a bid for sympathy, it was also a way of testing the group, to see how far they were willing to accept him as stable and rational, or whether they would turn and regard him and his outbursts as childish.

In the second place, the group, composed mainly of veteran ministers, gave their junior practical advice on how to find another job, and informed him of conditions in other dioceses.

Later in the session, they gave equally direct guidance on the way the curate should and should not approach his vestry. Here the group assumed a *supervisory* role, enabling Gosling to plan and rehearse strategy under the eye of his elders. The group may have been able thereby to prevent the young man from behaving impolitically in his future negotiations with his parish.

On a third level, the group provided a supportive setting within which Gosling could safely work off anger against his parish and against diocesan and national church organization. His hostile outbursts were absorbed and gradually restrained by the other ministers within realistic bounds. They constantly brought his complaints down out of the realm of hyperbole into a field of actual problems which they too shared. Gosling's frustrations were thus transmuted from a feeling of personal outrage and a "search for a son-of-a-bitch" into the potentially useful form of seeing his experience as part of larger issues affecting his whole profession, which could only be changed at a higher organizational level by corporate action.

This latter aspect of the session was also emotionally and cognitively useful for the other participants, since they too were able to ventilate similar frustrations and fears, to exchange information, and to promise each other support in altering the conditions that pressed on everyone.

Finally, on a fourth level, consultation took place. The understanding of the consultee and the group about the human relations and organizational dynamics of Gosling's case, and the number of possible options available to him, was expanded. The use of budgets by congregations as a method of controlling and retaliating against clergy was discussed. The group explored the ways in which "secret committees" can be approached, thus reducing the superstitious awe of some of the ministers about cabals that, they felt, controlled their fate.

Throughout the session, the group applied themselves exclusively to the problems of their profession, and specifically to helping Gosling to remain and succeed in the ministry. Yet within that framework, an effective and timely dose of emotional help was given.

chapter *8*

Evaluation

In their report *The Problems of the Priest*, based on the survey conducted in 1968 among 913 Episcopal ministers, the researchers concluded that "The parochial clergyman feels alone, unsupported, undertrained, underappreciated, and distinctly underpaid." [1] If consultation has any role to play in easing the strain and discontent of such men, as the clergy who first organized and nurtured the Massachusetts program intended, then it should be seen to focus on some of those areas where ministers feel the greatest pain.

Consultation must be fulfilling certain needs, since some of those who joined the program in its earliest stages have continued to attend meetings with notable regularity. They have done so despite annual changes in consultants, with the consequent need to adjust to new personalities and styles, and despite the fact that for some this has also meant long and inconvenient commuting, made all the more arduous by the driving conditions of Massachusetts winters.

In order to learn how its participants regard the program, we conducted an informal survey of all those who had enrolled during the first three years, and about half of these—twenty-two men—answered, most taking the trouble to comment in detail.

Thirteen men wrote that they were eager to participate further in consultation; four others were prepared to continue if certain conditions were met, like moving the place of meeting so that access from outlying areas of the diocese would be easier, or altering the frequency of sessions. Five men wrote that they would no longer attend. Of these, however, one was retiring, and wrote enthusiastically about his past experiences with the program, and two others felt that the meetings had been interesting but did not happen to fit their particular needs.

We asked the men if they could recall "instances in which talking about a case or a parish predicament with the consultant alone or in the group added to your understanding or otherwise improved your thinking about it." Seventeen ministers could recall such experiences and could describe the changes brought about in their thinking. The following is an example:

"One vivid recollection is the discussion of a woman living a rather empty life about whom there was an odor of potential suicide. The consultant was pointing out how this lady's life had been characterized by a whole series of losses of one kind or another. This sharpened my awareness of other such circumstances that I see people go through; and the potential for suicide is present there as well. The constant draining from a person's life of supportive relationships seems destined to drain him of his own value. I also remember somewhere along the line discovering that depression and anger were two facets of the same emotion. It seems simple enough, but it has been a very helpful discovery."

Another example: "I had one case concerning a young, strong-willed woman who attempted to take leadership in the parish woman's organization but who constantly called others and got them wound up (including the Rector) to the point that they and she would blow up. Actually, in talking this out, it was pointed out that she carried out her anger and frustration by upsetting others, and then standing back and watching the fireworks. In realizing this, I was able to overcome my hostility, in part, and attempt a new tack in my pastoral relations with her."

And another: "I had recently moved to my parish, and I was going through a miserable period with the vestry of my church. The greatest help (from consultation) in terms of insight was with regard to how to deal with a vestry that had been unable to transfer loyalties from the former rector."

And a final sampling: "Almost all the cases I presented were multiple problem cases in which I became deeply involved. The consultants and groups helped me to get a better picture of what was going on. It was a sort of 'couldn't see the forest for the trees' situation. The consultants were invaluable in helping me to understand the psychodynamics of the situations. They also helped me as far as my own expectations were concerned. I tend to be task-oriented and therefore feel I must produce definite results. I distinctly remember that in one situation I was advised that I should expect that mine would probably be a hand-holding role for ever and ever and that there was definite value in this because it probably would keep the lid on the boiling pot."

The men who responded to this survey, as well as others to whom we spoke, concluded that consultation gave them three major types of support. First, they appreciated the technical information that was offered by specialist consultants, and felt that they had learned a great deal about community mental health and about the nature and management of cases of mental disorder among their parishioners. They felt more self-assured in handling such people; and one man reported that his rate of referrals had dropped since he had realized that he could deal with a number of commonly occurring problems on his own or with the advice of a local specialist. Consultees also felt reassured that if they were to come across particularly complicated psychological cases, they would be able to get competent advice by the next group meeting, or even faster in an emergency, since consultation can be carried out by telephone.

A clergyman from an outlying parish, for example, phoned a consultant with the following story: The head of his Sunday school, a forty-five-year-old married man with three children, was sexually molesting little boys, and the minister wanted the psychiatrist to remove him from the parish as quickly as possible. The consultant asked for details, and learned that three years earlier, the man, while driving a teenage boy home from a church function, had put his hand on the boy's thigh. The boy had repulsed him angrily, and had then taken the story to his father. The father had reported the incident to the minister, and the minister had called on the teacher to explain. The man had admitted the charge, but said that he was having marital problems and was under strain. The minister told him to get psychiatric treatment, which the man agreed to do. There had been no further problems until a couple of days before the minister's call to the consultant, when the teacher had again touched the thigh of another teenager. The boy had hit him, and then had told his father, who was the most influential businessman in the community and a former vestryman. The father had come storming to the minister; and in the ensuing discussion, the rector mentioned the teacher's behavior three years earlier. The father now demanded that the teacher be discharged at once, saying to the minister, "*You* are on the hot seat. You have been warned twice. If there is another assault, it will be your responsibility!"

After drawing out further details, the consultant concluded that the man did not sound like a sex fiend, preying on little boys, but like someone who, on two occasions, three years apart, had made relatively mild advances to well-chosen victims, both of whom were athletic teenagers who could be expected to take care of themselves with little difficulty. The boys, in fact, had not only hit or abused the teacher, but they had mobilized the adults in the community against him. The latest "victim" had spread the story through the whole Sunday school, so that the principal was now regarded with contempt by all his pupils. The chance of his touching another child in this roused community was therefore slight.

The man's homosexual behavior, the consultant pointed out, could not be regarded as a disease but, rather, as a sign of lost control and as a call for help. What, he asked, could have happened recently in this man's life to trigger such behavior? The minister now remembered that, indeed, the man had been depressed for the past few weeks. He had just lost a part-time job and was in financial trouble. His wife had been forced to return to work, and this had produced tensions in their marriage. In addition, the teacher was engaged in a fight with the vestry over changes in the Sunday school curriculum.

"No wonder," the minister said, "the poor man is behaving like this."

The clergyman realized that instead of having a sex maniac on his hands, he had a rather ineffectual, unpopular middle-aged man under stress that made him doubt his masculinity. Moreover, the incident of three years before had shown that if the minister ordered the principal to get psychiatric help, the man would obey. Perhaps the best course of action during this episode, the consultant suggested, would be for the minister to refer the teacher again to a psychiatric clinic, while also giving pastoral counseling to him and his wife, and arranging to support the principal in his duties with the school. Once his stress was attenuated, the symptoms of that stress, the homosexual gestures, were likely to vanish too.

As for the irate father, the consultant advised the minister not to be unduly disturbed by his language of shock and outrage. Rather, the rector might tell him that he had consulted the psychiatrist, and that the latter doubted whether there would be more trouble, but was now sharing the responsibility should there be any further "assaults." The minister was considerably relieved.

This entire process took less than fifteen minutes on a telephone. In that time, the consultant helped the minister to reappraise an apparently desperate case, and to reduce it to manageable terms. As a result, the minister was not only relieved of much of his worry, but was now able to help the principal to recover normal control over his impulses, and to reduce the isolation from his community that might have created more serious acts of deviance in the future.

Some consultees felt that one of the greatest benefits of consultation lay in the support it gave them not only in emergencies, but also in bearing up under their load of chronic cases. They could raise such cases periodically in order to be reassured that they were doing whatever was possible, and to understand why there had or had not been any new developments in the lives of these parishioners. In reference to such periodic consultation, in this instance about an alcoholic woman, one clergyman said: "It keeps me from getting discouraged and saying, 'I'm just a failure as a counselor.' It also stops me from taking the other tack and saying, 'Oh, she's impossible! I can't help her, so she can go hang. She's determined to commit suicide by slow degrees, so let her do it!' I think it's vital not to fall into either one of these positions."

Another man, who needed a way of maintaining objectivity and flexibility with irritating "regular customers," said: "I say in my sermons, 'God means us to love everybody'; and it seems like fifteen minutes after I've said it, He sends me someone to make me prove it.

"There's a very sick man in my parish who's been a real problem for years. He's very arrogant and offensive, always putting on acts and strutting about, and he drives the church secretaries and the curates wild. Whenever we see his car in the driveway, we all think, 'Oh, dear, here we go again!' The only thing that prevents me from literally saying, 'You are *not* welcome inside these doors! We have done all we can for you, and nobody can help you,' is the fact that I can keep bringing up this particular case for consultation."

The second area where the program gave significant benefit, consultees felt, was that the meetings provided a setting where they were brought together with colleagues. As each case was discussed, men who might have thought that they were laboring under unique burdens found that they had much in common and that, consequently, they were not abnormal, nor was their situation peculiar. One man wrote that consultation "was tremendously helpful, therapeutic and healing to me. There was repeatedly a sense of community support. I realized that I do not fail alone—dozens of other clergymen are equally frustrated and as helpless as I am. . . . I . . . found myself looking forward to the refreshment and strengthening experience of group participation and involvement. It had sabbath overtones of rest, insight, strength-acceptance."

Not only does such sharing increase self-confidence; it also reduces the loneliness of the minister's profession, to which the authors of *The Problems of the Priest* refer: "The parish priest has a lonely job—with serious and varied responsibilities. . . . He sees no clear-cut support systems, or guidelines from which he may take cues. He must do battle with the problems of his day-to-day ministry on his own."

At first sight, many consultees seemed to have the companionship of colleagues. They come from communities where there is a strong ecumenical spirit, and where they meet with clergymen of other denominations, and not infrequently collaborate with them in joint projects. These contacts, however, appear to be less effective as supports than sharing experiences with fellow Episcopalians. Some of the comfort that men derive from consultation comes from the informal gossip about diocesan organization, personalities, and politics that takes place before and after the meetings, as well as from the fellowship they sustain. In addition, ministers get concrete guidance in professional predicaments from fellow Episcopal clergy, whose parish situation is similar to their own and who are often confronted by analogous problems. Through discussions in the group and outside it about such issues, for example, as how to accustom a congregation to the modernized liturgy, individual ministers were able to explore vicariously a variety of options for action. Consequently, each minister was not forced to experiment with every logical possibility, but could restrict himself to those paths that others had found promising.

Many ministers, knowing the tendency of their colleagues to snipe at each other and to engage in sharp rivalries, wondered at first how safe it would be to reveal their weaknesses by presenting a case with which they were having difficulties for the inspection of other clergy. In actual experience, however, it was rare for any disparaging to take place, whatever men's private opinions might have been on the performance of their colleagues. As one rather acerbic man said: "Whenever I feel like saying to someone, 'Boy, that was a dumb move,' I remember that I may be giving the next case and looking just as stupid. And you know, it's odd. Some people whom you've always thought of as pretty incompetent turn out to have handled things remarkably well. You learn a lot about your neighbours at these groups. Some of the most unexpected people have real wisdom."

Most of the ministers concluded that one of the most valuable aspects of the program lay in the insights it gave them into the work of their neighbors; and they realized, perhaps for the first time, the extent of their colleagues' abilities. Case discussions, said one minister, "revealed how similar (although differing in frequency of occurrence in different parishes) the pastoral problems were with which we had to deal. They revealed with what sympathy and responsiveness the various clergy—differing so much from one another in other attributes—all tried to deal with these problems, thereby building up legitimate professional pride (otherwise often badly eroded among parish clergy these days). . . . Consultation reemphasized the importance of our work. In a profession, most of whose members work alone, with little time or energy left over for other than recreational associations with their colleagues (and less of that as the years go on), this program would fill

some of the needs—in terms of clarifying perspective and raising professional morale—performed in more financially pros-
perous professions by specialist conferences."

A few men appeared to have attended literally dozens of sessions without ever presenting cases of their own—drawn, apparently, to the companionship of the group. Consultation,
one of these ministers wrote, "was a way to become better ac-
quainted with a small group of clergymen plus improving our
knowledge." Another wrote, "It is *very* helpful to discuss with
one's peers the pastoral problems related to the ministry. Although one may not have had the same problem presented at
his doorstep, it is helpful to think them all through."

Some men reported looking forward to meetings as one of
their few opportunities to talk regularly with intellectual
equals. They came from areas where the only topics of conversation seemed to be parish business, the local gossip, or records
of sports teams; while in the groups, they found an opportunity to exercise their minds with more abstract topics.

Paradoxically, this sense of companionship was buttressed
by the fact that what were brought forward at these meetings
were cases in which ministers were threatened with failure.
The group then made a concerted effort to rescue a colleague
from his predicament, and this led to considerable friendliness
on both sides. This produced a different atmosphere from that
which arose in a group organized by ministers in another area,
in which members were asked to share innovations they had
developed for managing common problems of administration
and counseling. It was found, however, that this threatened
and further depressed those members of the group to whom
bright ideas did not come readily, and who felt even more inadequate as they listened to the techniques discovered by more
inventive neighbors.

Consultation groups also improved morale by providing for
alternation between the role of helper and the role of one seeking help, since the man who presented a case at one session

would offer his insights to an equally perplexed friend at the following meeting. Thus a man had no need to worry about showing blind spots, since he would be revealed as an objective, wise adviser when someone else presented a case.

The third source of support was more subtle. It was the "reference group" created by the culture of the consultation program and embodied in the values and traditions of the regular meetings of the group. This had special supportive meaning over and above the personal actions of the individual participants. Men seemed to identify with a total endeavor that had continuity, that was the bearer of specific values, that prescribed a particular style of wrestling with confusing problems —insisting, for example, on toleration of ambiguity, rather than allowing rapid, simplified conclusions that might be more comfortable for the minister, but which inevitably distort reality, and the impact of which was regularly renewed by the weekly meetings. The effect of this may be analogous, in psychosocial terms, to the spiritual support derived from regular meetings of a religious communion.

Similar experiences were reported by the fourteen wives of clergy consultees who requested their own consultation group. This group met a number of times, resolved to continue, but petered out for lack of administrative leadership. Two women rated this program as "not helpful"; the rest felt that the meetings had been supportive. They met other clergy wives, whom many had previously stereotyped as people they would not want to mix with, but with whom they found, on the contrary, that they could share common doubts and problems. They now saw that the bishop and his staff regarded them as significant and worthy of help, since the diocese was prepared to sponsor such a program for them. They discussed ways of handling the anger and frustration generated by certain aspects of their role; they talked of the burdens imposed by their communities' expectations about them and their children; and they shared problems created by low salaries.

While many of the women wondered whether they wanted to go on meeting with a psychiatric consultant, they felt, nevertheless, that they had gained self-confidence from the presence of someone who could assure them that their reactions to the stress of their role were "healthy." "I'm glad to find out that my feelings do not indicate that I have mental health problems," one woman said.

Within the men's group, an atmosphere was also created in which it was possible to ventilate resentment and hostility. It was common for men to voice anger at vestries, the diocesan administration, or individual parishioners, and for this to be accepted by their fellows, who nevertheless limited such expressions to reasonable bounds. Usually, hostility came out as jocular remarks. One minister said of a psychotic woman who persisted in phoning him at impossible hours, "I didn't want to hang up on her, but I felt, if she goes on talking long enough, maybe she'll go bankrupt, and then the phone company will rip out her phone!" This was greeted with complete understanding by men who had had similar experiences in the early hours of the morning and had felt just as aggrieved.

The attractiveness of consultation for many of its participants was increased by the fact that it could be entered into at low emotional cost. In order to mobilize the supportive and educational services of the program, ministers needed to cross only a low threshold. Unlike other support systems which are now in fashion, consultation has no cultic aspect. It requires no act of faith or commitment on the part of the participant to be effective. Those groups which do require such an emotional investment create a situation where the stakes are high. The program itself becomes a test case for commitment and trust of one's fellows, and if the experience is disappointing, the ensuing disillusionment may extend beyond that system to a generalized sense of defeat and betrayal of trust.

Consultation, on the other hand, is emotionally safe and cool. If the minister does not find a session useful, he has only lost an hour to boredom; he has not sustained any damage to his faith in himself or in human nature. Occasionally, even failures in consultation can be soothing. As could be seen in the case of Waters, if a minister brings a troublesome case to a specialist, and the specialist is at a loss, the consultee and his parishioner may not be much advanced, but at least the clergyman is relieved of some of his sense of inadequacy if even the specialist consultant cannot see any immediate solution.

Some of the ministers who responded to the survey, however, were by no means satisfied or complimentary. One felt that he had been helped "only to a small degree. In general I found discussion tended only to support and reinforce my own method of dealing with cases. In a few situations, the consultant was helpful in pointing out some possible behavior patterns I was not aware of, e.g., 'frigidity.' " But on the whole, this man concluded, "I felt that the consultant allowed the group to dwell too much on the specifics of individual cases, rather than using them as models for consideration or counseling techniques, and discussion of the relative merits of various approaches to pastoral cases."

Another wrote of his reservations about the program: "I think one of the problems here is the long wait before you have a chance to put in your two cents' worth. You listen to a very complex, condensed story of someone known intimately to another, and then you are asked to comment on it, and one of the things that baffles you is how to pick up some of the pieces of the story so that you can go on from there. At times, I felt that it was a hopeless situation. At other times, I marveled at the patience and perseverance of the rector. But not very often could I tune in to the particulars and really give any advice. Somehow, the setting or perhaps I was at fault. I regret to give such a negative report. I trust the others felt differently."

A third respondent was more critical, and concluded: "Some of the clergy were so unperceptive about the problems they faced that much time was wasted (from *my* point of view).

The psychiatrist bent over backwards to be so polite and non-judgmental that it was unreal. Stupidity was accepted too freely. Generally, the sessions tended to be a pooling of ignorance unless rescued by the psychiatrist. The clergy quality was quite mixed, with many of the more verbal members the ones who contributed least."

Finally, a man who had attended ten sessions before declining to participate further, wrote: "We are not social workers or junior psychologists and when the leader of the program admits that he knows nothing about religion or the part it plays in one's life then the program is of little value to people who are religiously oriented."

Other clergymen, however, felt that there had been a major benefit precisely in working with consultants who were not "religiously oriented," for this, as one minister pointed out, constituted external validation. Clergy who doubted the efficacy of their own work were now assured not only by their peers, but also by members of another profession—who may even have belonged to another religion—that what they were doing did indeed have real value, and did fulfill a need in community life.

A veteran consultee summed up his experiences with the program: "There were no great miracles, but there was a softening of tensions." Another put his impressions this way: "In consultation, they treat you as though you are sane. It's so refreshing."

chapter 9

Implications for Community Mental Health

Gerald Caplan

In this chapter I will deal with two topics. First, I will describe some further developments of our program—after its inception as an effort to help parish clergy—beginning with consultation to the Bishop of Massachusetts, followed by a countrywide program in the Episcopal Church through its House of Bishops, and finally to the possible beginnings of a similar national program in the United Methodist Church. Second, I will discuss the implications of our experience for community mental health theory, and I will propose a conceptual model to guide mental health workers in the development of effective collaboration with human-service organizations.

My remarks are addressed primarily to community mental health specialists, but I hope that they will also be of interest and of value to clergymen and other caregivers in line with the fundamental purpose of this book which attempts to act as a facilitator of communication among all of us who desire to work together to improve the mental health of the people in our communities.

CONSULTATION TO THE BISHOP

In Chapter 1 Ruth Caplan has presented an account of the development of our consultation program in Massachusetts. I

167

will here amplify this by describing what took place in my consultation to Bishop Stokes and his staff.

I arranged with Bishop Stokes that my first few sessions at his headquarters should take the form of meetings with him alone, so that he might instruct me about the history and traditions of the Episcopal Church and about the day-to-day realities of his duties and responsibilities as a bishop. He gave me a number of books and memoranda to read, as well as the Constitution and Canons of the diocese; and we had a series of fascinating interviews, made all the more interesting to both of us because I knew little about the Episcopal Church, and the bishop had the task of explaining things to me that he had long taken for granted, but now was able to look at in a new light as he empathized with my efforts to understand them.

This was the first time that I had talked at length with a bishop, and at first I was rather anxious in this unfamiliar setting. Bishop Stokes quickly put me at my ease, and in doing so overcame his own anxiety—this was the first time that he had talked at length to a psychiatrist and had been obliged to give a detailed explanation of his religion and his role to an outsider. We developed a warm relationship of mutual trust and respect, but it was not until a year later that we confessed to each other how strained we had both been during our initial meetings. Although the original plan had called for headquarters' sessions every three or four weeks, we soon developed a rhythm of meeting at intervals of two weeks; and in the third year of our program we met every seven to ten days as I helped the bishop clarify the many complicated issues involved in planning for his retirement and for preparing the field for his successor.

Bishop Stokes soon discovered that he could derive great benefit from our consultation discussions, so much so that he was unwilling to forego any of them for group meetings between me and his headquarters' staff as had been envisioned originally by the clergymen's planning committee. Instead, we worked out the interesting pattern of calling in one or more of the staff to our regular sessions, as work problems in which they were involved became salient in consultation. The particular benefit of this format was that I never had to be concerned about preserving confidentiality regarding staff communications to me in my subsequent discussions with the bishop, since he was present throughout all our interviews. Over the three years of my consultations with Bishop Stokes I got to know in this way all members of his staff in relation to specific work problems; and, in addition, the bishop also invited into some of our sessions leading laymen who happened to be involved in diocesan organizational issues that we were jointly studying.

Much of my consultation to the bishop focused on helping him clarify complications of his multiple role segments: as the administrator of a large and busy organization; as the *pastor pastorum*, the spiritual and pastoral counselor of his clergy and their families; as the religious authority and liturgical head of his church; as a leader involved in grappling with a constant succession of emergent social problems involving not only his own church but the larger community; and as the organizer and chairman of the Diocesan Council and Convention. Each of our consultations lasted for two hours; and usually we discussed several issues, some of which the bishop had prepared ahead of time and others that emerged spontaneously as we talked.

We discussed in detail cases of individual clergymen and their families whom the bishop was called upon to counsel in regard to emotional problems or illness, marital difficulties, alcoholism, adjustment problems, etc. We spent considerable time dealing with rectors or curates who were having problems with their vestry, or vice versa. We talked about persons who had to leave their jobs for one reason or another, age, illness, unsuitability for a particular parish, and the like; we analyzed the many factors involved in finding an appropriate job or retraining opportunity for each one, and also discussed possible ways of organizing improved clergy selection and redeployment procedures for the diocese. We discussed the problems of the newly appointed clergymen and the even more difficult problems of those who retire. On a couple of occasions we dealt with vexing disciplinary problems involving clergymen who had transgressed the code of their religious calling. We discussed community organizational problems in certain parishes divided by factional disputes. Our consultations also dealt with the bishop's strategic and tactical planning of the annual conventions, and with his management of the relations between his clergy and the lay leadership of the diocese.

Above all, we discussed in many different forms the question of the morale of the parish clergy; and we worked out a variety of ways for the bishop to support them in mastering the challenges of their roles as community leaders and personal counselors for their parishioners, such as personal visits by the bishop to their homes and to their vestry meetings; social gatherings in the bishop's home for ministers and their wives; a discussion group for wives; district meetings for groups of clergymen; support for continuation education; and the development of policies to facilitate support among parish clergy. The major technical problem that continually burdened us emerged from the fact that the diocese includes 186 churches. The bishop is, therefore, not able to visit any parish systematically more than about once in three years. On the other hand, the most potent support to the parish clergyman comes from an individual personal interaction between him and his bishop; and intermediaries such as archdeacons, canons, and suffragan bishops, while helpful, are less than perfect alternatives. We never did develop a completely satisfactory solution to this problem, although we discussed ways whereby the bishop could maintain a continuing diocesewide supportive structure through regular printed messages and through acts of leadership in publicized responses to church and general community dilemmas and challenges, such as issues of race relations, the Vietnam War, student unrest, anti-poverty programs, and urban renewal.

The role of a bishop or other top-level denominational administrator is a lonely one. Not only is he a chief executive in a hierarchical organization, but the religious and pastoral aspects of his position make it hard for him to share his professional perplexities and leadership dilemmas with his followers and dependents. Bishop Stokes often spoke with appreciation of the opportunity provided by consultation with an objective and understanding outsider to relieve some of this role loneliness, and to have a structure within which he could reflect calmly about cognitively difficult and emotionally taxing predicaments. He also emphasized the feeling of personal security that he derived from the task orientation of our discussions— we never transgressed our ground rules that private and personal matters should be kept out of our interviews, even during our final consultations about his impending retirement and the problems of his handing over the reins of office to Bishop John Burgess, who had been his suffragan for several years.

THE HOUSE OF BISHOPS' PROGRAM

During the second year of our Massachusetts program, Bishop Stokes asked me whether I would talk to a colleague of his from the House of Bishops, Bishop David E. Richards, who had recently returned to this country from service in Costa Rica and who was interested in mental health work in the church. When Bishop Richards came to see me, he told me that he was now staffing the Pastoral Development Committee of the House of Bishops, which was investigating what bishops could do to promote the mental health of their clergymen and to assist the latter in counseling their parishioners. At a recent meeting of his committee, Bishop Stokes had reported briefly on our program in Massachusetts, and the members of his

committee had asked Bishop Richards to find out more about
it.

At that stage, I knew very little about the national organizational structure of the Episcopal Church, and in response to
my questions Bishop Richards told me that the House of Bishops, consisting of about 120 diocesan, coadjutor, and suffragan
bishops from all the dioceses of the Americas, under the chair-
manship of the Presiding Bishop, has great responsibility for
guiding the affairs of the American Episcopal Church. The
Pastoral Development Committee was one of a series of units
of the House of Bishops appointed to implement its pastoral
concerns for the church's clergy.

After I had explained the theoretical background of our
mental health consultation approach and discussed our Harvard experience with other caregiving systems such as schools
and public-health agencies over many years, as well as our
work during the previous two years with the Massachusetts
Diocese, Bishop Richards asked whether I would be willing to
come to the next meeting of his committee in Philadelphia to
talk about our ideas. I agreed, and two months later I attended the Philadelphia meeting, where I discussed our program with ten bishops from different parts of the country.

This meeting rapidly developed into a consultation session,
in which the committee solicited my collaboration in working
out their own program. They said that our Massachusetts
work was most interesting and should be publicized so that it
might be replicated in other dioceses where properly qualified
mental health consultants might be available; and they asked
me to help Bishop Richards, and any diocese that requested
his help in setting up such a program, to locate consultants
who were skilled in this kind of work. But they then moved on
to a topic that was of greater and more immediate interest to
their committee. They told me that they were currently trying
to develop programs to provide support for bishops. Fostering
the professional and spiritual well-being of bishops was a cen-

tral mission of the House of Bishops, and they had been charged to deal with this as part of the overall mandate of their committee. They felt that since the bishop was the key executive in each diocese, his mental health and his understanding of the psychosocial aspects of his role would surely exert a major influence on the social structure and culture of his diocese and hence on the well-being and effectiveness of his clergy in working with their parishioners.

As we continued discussing this issue, it became clear to me that although the bishops were sincerely appreciative of the merits of our program in Massachusetts they did not believe that it was likely to be replicated in many other dioceses, partly because of the difficulty of finding expert consultants and partly because it would involve bishops in turning for help to outside experts, and particularly to mental health specialists, in regard to sensitive internal matters of their church and their own roles. The committee appeared to be searching for a way of dealing with the problems of bishops by some service inside the church, in line with the dominant philosophy of their House of Bishops. Eventually, one of them asked me whether I thought that the kind of consultation I had been giving Bishop Stokes might not, instead, be provided by another bishop. This led to a discussion of the transferability of consultation skills from clinical to nonclinical professions and the pros and cons of outside versus inside consultants.

Our discussion then moved to a consideration of the simpler question of whether I could communicate to the members of the committee in a short seminar the basic elements of our Harvard population-oriented preventive psychiatry approach so that they could utilize this knowledge in their own dioceses and also in their planning of programs for other bishops. I readily agreed and we arranged for a three-day seminar in Massachusetts on community mental health principles, to be attended by members of the committee and other bishops who might be interested.

A couple of months later we held our community mental health seminar in Cambridge, Massachusetts, and it turned out to be a meeting of considerable importance. It was attended by about twenty bishops, and we used my book, *Principles of Preventive Psychiatry* (New York: Basic Books, 1964) as our text. I focused my presentations mainly on crisis theory and on ways of organizing services to help people master life crises effectively so that they might improve their future mental health. In this connection I discussed techniques of anticipatory guidance and preventive intervention to individuals and their families during crisis periods, and also ways of mobilizing support for such people by the caregiving professionals of their community, with particular reference to the potential role of clergymen. Within this context I talked about mental health consultation and other forms of helpful collaboration between clergymen and mental health specialists.

Following my initial presentations, we began a discussion of practical possibilities for implementing these ideas within the Episcopal Church, and my role changed from educator to consultant as our entire group moved toward working out plans for possible new programs in the church. A series of recommendations began to emerge that would be referred for implementation by Bishop Richards and his Pastoral Development Committee, most of whose members were present at the seminar.

First, it was decided that the Massachusetts consultation program should be widely publicized as a model that other dioceses might wish to utilize. Second, our group decided that a manual should be compiled for new bishops, to provide them with information about administrative and organizational aspects of their role, with particular reference to establishing a structure in their dioceses that would promote the well-being of parish clergy and would support them by means of in-service education, supervision and consultation in their front-line counseling work with emotionally disturbed parishioners, and in the other psychosocial aspects of parish work.

The third and most interesting recommendation was that the House of Bishops should set up an experimental program for consultation by experienced bishops to newly appointed bishops in order to help them master the crises of their first two years of office, and to assist them professionally in establishing a suitable support structure for their parish clergy. I agreed to organize a three-day seminar on consultation techniques for a selected group of senior bishops, who after this training would offer themselves as consultants to newly appointed colleagues. I also agreed to assist Bishop Richards to supervise this program both by means of occasional telephone consultations to bishop-consultants who might be encountering unusual problems in technique and through regular one-day or two-day supervisory group meetings once or twice a year.

A few weeks later I went with Bishop Richards, Bishop Stokes, and the chairman of the Pastoral Development Committee to talk about these recommendations with the Presiding Bishop in New York. He accepted the plan, promised his administrative support, and said he would like to attend the consultation-training session himself.

The following year we held our first three-day consultation-training session, attended by twenty-three bishops, and we discussed not only consultation techniques but also the practical details of our experimental program, which became known as "Bishop-to-Bishop Coordinate Status Consultation." It was significant that the style of consultation that emerged, although clearly based upon the method I had described to the group as being the one used by mental health clinicians, was different in important ways, particularly due to the fact that the consultant bishop was a senior member of the same profession as his consultee. Techniques for ensuring that the latter would not feel threatened or coerced to accept the spoken or implied advice of his consultant, but, as in traditional mental health consultation, would be free to reject any element of it and thus retain his full professional autonomy, became a central issue. Hence the words "Coordinate Status" in the title

that the bishops chose for their method are of special importance. In our discussions that led to the evolution of the new
techniques, I took care to act as a facilitator and resource person to the group and not to obtrude ideas based upon my own
experience with clinician consultants. The bishops tailored the
emerging method to their own resources and situation.

In this connection I was fascinated to discover that although
the bishops often used a different vocabulary from clinicians,
their level of psychological insight and interpersonal skill was
not inferior to that of clinicians. For instance, as part of my
lecture, I showed the bishops a documentary film of a psychiatrist conducting a consultation interview with a public-health
nurse, which I often use as a vehicle for training clinicians in
mental health consultation. The film is a good training instrument, because it deals with a complicated case that poses
many interesting problems in consultation technique. There
are a number of red herrings in the manifest content, and the
underlying themes are not easy for beginning consultants to
identify. I had been hesitant about showing this film to the
bishops, because I felt that to realize its inner implications one
would need a deep understanding of unconscious processes
that would demand a clinical background and experience. To
my surprise, as soon as the film was over the bishops immediately launched into a sophisticated discussion of the various
unconscious psychological factors manifested by the consultant
and consultee; and although some of them modestly expressed
the opinion that a bishop could never hope to become as skillful as the psychiatrist in the film, it was obvious that the level
of their theoretical analysis was in no way lower than what I
usually encountered among clinicians to whom I had shown
the film. My surprise at this indicated to me that I had still not
quite overcome the traditional stereotyped derogatory attitudes of a clinician in evaluating the psychological insight of
members of other professions. By today, after nearly two years'
experience with the bishops' consultation program, I do be-

lieve that my original stereotypes are quite dissipated, and I have come to the sincere realization that clergymen have the professional capacity to become as skillful in consultation techniques as mental health clinicians.

At the end of the seminar, Bishop Richards called for members to join the first cadre of consultants, and we worked out a suggested procedure for setting up the new program. We agreed that we would meet again after a few months to discuss consultation techniques in further detail, and we hoped that meanwhile the first consultations would have taken place and reports about them might be used as case materials in our seminar discussions. But when we convened the seminar again, we discovered that only a few people had volunteered to become consultants, and that because of administrative obstacles only three consultations had actually taken place. However, an indication that we were moving in the right direction was afforded by the fact that twenty-four bishops attended the second three-day training seminar, and that the Presiding Bishop himself participated for one of the days. Since he is a very busy man indeed, his presence validated for me and for the bishops that our program was likely to be acceptable to the church.

During the following year the new program began to take hold: nineteen consultant-consultee pairs were established, and in addition to the continuing staff work by Bishop Richards, I ran a one-day supervisory group attended by eight of the consultants. At that meeting we began to grapple with problems of recording the consultation process and the associated difficulty of preserving confidentiality in supervisory discussions in an organization as small and intimate as the Episcopal Church where the only person present who was not able to penetrate the disguising of the identity of the consultees was likely to be me. We also began to work out the details of the overall agreements between consultees and consultants so as to develop a uniform structure in the program, which would eventually provide an opportunity for evaluation. The members decided that future supervisory group meetings should last two days and that we should base them mainly on the discussion of case vignettes that would illustrate typical problems of technique. We also decided that since the program was proving to be so popular we would offer the opportunity of becoming a consultant to any bishop who was willing to attend a three-day training session and the follow-up supervisory sessions. In this way, we hoped to avoid the development in the House of Bishops of an elitist, closed-group reputation for the consultants, and to further our objective of building an open, nonpolitical, supportive network within the church.

At the time of writing, this fascinating new program seems to be developing well. In April and May of 1972, I expect to direct a two-day supervisory seminar for twenty active consultant bishops and a three-day didactic seminar for an equal number of bishops who wish to join up as new consultants. The Presiding Bishop offers all newly consecrated bishops in the church the opportunity to receive consultation from a senior colleague whom they may choose from our list of consultants. So far, almost every newly appointed bishop has accepted the offer, and we have been able to provide enough bishop consultants to follow through with the program.

POSSIBLE BEGINNINGS WITH THE UNITED METHODIST CHURCH

At our second consultation training two Methodist bishops participated as observers. They had heard about our program and felt that it might be of value as a model for their own church, which was currently grappling with similar problems. At the end of the seminar, the visitors expressed much appreciation for what we were doing, and one of them, the Bishop of New England, asked whether I would be willing to organize a program for him similar to that which we were offering to Bishop Burgess and the Episcopal Diocese of Massachusetts. I replied that I would be pleased to discuss the matter further, although from the few details he gave me about the pattern of organization of his church it seemed that we would have to develop a somewhat different type of program, because the United Methodist Church is, nationally, about three times the size of the Episcopal Church and is organized into much larger geographical units.

During the following year I heard nothing further from the Bishop of New England; and then Bishop Richards told me that he had been invited to a meeting of the Methodist Council of Bishops to describe our Bishop-to-Bishop Consultation program and to discuss the possibility of the Methodists establishing a similar countrywide program in their church. Bishop Richards consulted with me the day before that meeting to plan his presentation, and later he reported that he had been well received, and that the Methodist bishops intended to set up an experimental program of attaching a senior bishop to advise each newly appointed bishop in their church along lines similar to the program of the Episcopal Church. But they were not convinced that their senior bishops needed to spend the time and energy to learn special consultation techniques. These men were already highly experienced in dealing with people and in operating in counseling and pastoral roles, and some of them felt that they might manage just as well dealing with the communication and interpersonal relationship problems they would encounter in their traditional ways rather than trying to develop and learn a series of novel techniques. They intended to continue their discussion of this question and to keep in touch with us.

THEORETICAL CONSIDERATIONS

Introduction: The field of community mental health has not yet reached so advanced a stage of scientific development that it has been able to accumulate a comprehensive body of theory consisting of a systematic structure of articulating hypotheses that have been tested, or are capable of being tested, by determining whether they yield predictions that can be repeatedly validated. Our field is still at an earlier scientific stage, where the appropriate contribution of researchers takes the form of a meticulous natural history-type description of the unfolding of significant events, followed by the elaboration of simple conceptualizations that abstract the inner meaning of the described processes in order to form models. The latter serve to mold our expectations that similar patterns will occur in situations which differ in place, time, and person, but which may be recognized to be analogous in respect to their essential elements. Such models, developed by one researcher on the basis of his own experiences, may then guide other researchers or practitioners, so that they may order their data collection, their planning, and their interventions in patterns that lend meaning to observation of selected aspects of their field and allow the workers to predict expectable consequences from their actions.

It is within such a theoretical framework that I present the following ideas derived from the program so far described.

Conceptual Model: The central model that emerges from my consideration of our data, and that fits my other experiences in similar situations, is that one effective way for a community mental health agency to fulfill its mission of improving the human-relations aspects of the operations of a caregiving organization is to start working with one of its peripheral units, demonstrate mutually satisfying collaboration, develop a good reputation, and then move to higher and more central levels of the organizational structure, thus reaching successively wider populations. At each stage, the mental health workers offer their specialized input as a constructive contribution to the development of projects that are primarily tailored by the personnel of the organization to meet their own currently felt needs; and therefore the pattern of the projects and the particular contribution of the mental health workers is likely to vary significantly from level to level, rather than being a multiplication on a wider scale of what was found to be valuable at earlier stages of the program.

Thus at the peripheral level in Massachusetts what has proved satisfying and helpful to the parish clergy has been the group consultation described in the body of this book. This type of operation has also made sense to community mental health specialists. It still needs to be evaluated. It should be shown to improve the mental health of large numbers of parishioners as a result of more skillful work by ministers who have received consultation in these groups. But our analysis of the group transactions persuades us that this is a likely consequence because of the similarity of the picture to other experiences that the traditions of our profession define to be positive. This is far from scientific validation, but at the present stage of our professional development it is the best yardstick that practitioners have available.

At the level of the Bishop of Massachusetts a different pattern of collaboration occurred. Looking back, it is clear to me that I behaved wisely in agreeing readily to the bishop's suggestion that I meet alone with him for individual consultation, rather than repeating our pattern of group consultation with his headquarters' staff. This facilitated his development of the plan to bring his staff into our consultation interviews one or two at a time when their participation seemed appropriate.

At the level of the Pastoral Development Committee of the House of Bishops my formal consultation was restricted to the one group session in Philadelphia. From that developed my role as educator in seminars on community mental health and consultation techniques, and my ongoing collaboration with Bishop Richards in planning and implementing the Bishop-to-Bishop program. Once again, the innovative project that

emerged from my consultation was developed by my consultees—true, as a direct outcome of my help; but not at all on the
basis of a specific suggestion by me. It will be recalled that the
germs of the idea appeared in a question posed by one of the
bishops at the Philadelphia meeting; and that the plan itself
was crystallized during our first community mental health
seminar in Cambridge.

  Significance of Reputation: The importance of building a
"reputation" is an essential element in this model. My movement from level to level was not the result of a painstaking
replication of the original pattern in other analogous subsys-
tems of the organization. That is, I did not repeat our Massachusetts program in other dioceses; although I hope that as a
result of the publication of this book other similar programs of
group consultation to parish clergy and individual consultation to bishops and other top denominational administrators
will be organized wherever skilled mental health consultants
are available. Our model envisages a telescoping or skipping of
phases. Once a program and its workers have acquired a favorable reputation, the way is opened up for them to move
rapidly to upper levels of organization, and later to other organizations.

  In this respect three issues seem to have been important.
First, our original site of operations was highly visible and influential. I still know little about the history and traditions of
the Episcopal Church, but although I believe that all its dioceses are supposed to be of equal importance, I have the impression that some of them, because of size, wealth, and history, enjoy more prestige than others; and that certain bishops
have earned unusual respect, so that what they do and how
they think are particularly likely to command widespread attention. It was not an unimportant matter in the unfolding of
our program that the Diocese of Massachusetts and its bishops
have played a leadership role in the church; so that when
Bishop Stokes reported on his favorable experience with men-

tal health consultation it had more impact than if, for example, a report of an equally promising project in a less influential setting had been published as an article in a church or mental health journal.

Second, the reputation our program quickly gained in the Episcopal Church was enhanced by our preexisting national and international status in the community mental health field and by the prestige of Harvard University.

Starting Date: Third, the program was timely. Had it been started ten years earlier there would not have been the same intensity of felt need among church leaders that impelled them to invest resources and energy in helping bishops foster the mental health work of parish clergy. For that matter, our Massachusetts program did not begin in earlier years, although our Harvard group has been offering consultation for twenty years to school systems and public-health departments in our region. There is also nothing new in the idea that clergymen and religious organizations should play an important role in community mental health. The significant issue in the rapid development of our own program and in the potency of our reputation as an energizer of that development is that a succession of recent historical events, both inside the Episcopal Church and in the communities that it serves, have raised the salience of the mental health role of the minister and of the urgent need to undertake important organizational action in dealing with the problem of mental disorder in the population.

We may also speculate that if we had tried to start our Massachusetts program a few years later, it would probably not have been able to get off the ground. Two years later Bishop Stokes was preparing to retire and almost certainly would not have been willing to start a new program that might not be acceptable to his successor. The following two years were a period of reorganization of the central administration of the diocese, so that new programs have been encountering expectable difficulties, and we would have suffered in like manner.

From these considerations it would appear by hindsight that we had very little leeway in the date of starting a program that was likely to succeed locally and then rapidly spread to the church as a whole. What guidance, therefore, does our model offer a mental health specialist in deciding when to initiate a local action with the hope that it will start a sequence of events such as we have described? In other words, does our model have any predictive and prescriptive value, or is it just a *post hoc* explication of what has already taken place?

That is a difficult question to answer on the basis of a single case which has turned out so far to be apparently successful. In fact, of course, the model did not emerge in my mind as a new set of ideas derived solely from my analysis of the present program, but is rooted in years of experience with many caregiving organizations. My analysis of the present case has allowed me to make a clearer exposition of the model than ever before and to link it to a succession of concrete events, so that, hopefully, it will seem plausible to mental health specialists, some of whom may wish to adapt it to guide their own work and thus test it out in their different settings. The more important point is that the apparent success of the current case is itself a validation for me of a set of concepts that had been emerging from my previous experience and that guided me throughout my work with the Episcopal Church. It may already have been obvious from the story that I was behaving in accordance with a consistent set of principles in my efforts to build this program, principles that are consonant with my conceptual model.

Salience and Feasibility: Only in one area was I apparently not being guided by this model. Why did I start the program when I did? Why did I choose to spend so much time talking with the psychiatric resident about his volunteer church activities, as described in Chapter 1? There is little in the model that I have so far presented that could have helped me to answer these questions. What did help me was another set of concepts which it would not be appropriate to present in detail in this chapter, but which I have fully described elsewhere.[1] Briefly, I believe that a community mental health specialist should continually monitor his community to identify the caregiving organizations that are currently salient for his own mission, because they are catering to sections of the population who have an increased risk of becoming emotionally disordered and also because they are in a position to reduce that risk by ameliorating the pathogenic pressures of people's living conditions or by providing resources to help people master their difficulties so that they do not break down psychiatrically. The salience of a particular organization will vary over time because of changes in living patterns of the population and because of alterations in the problems that are considered burdensome in that community. Salience alone, however, should not determine with which organizations the community mental health specialist will spend his time. He must also be guided by rating the most salient agencies of his community in respect to their *feasibility* to be influenced by him so as to improve their mental health contributions to populations at risk. Feasibility implies openness to his entry, acceptance of his collaboration, possession of sufficient resources of leadership and staff so that improvement is possible, and manifesting enough organizational stability so that the improvements may be lasting.

A community mental health worker who is guided by these concepts will be continually watching developments in the salience and feasibility of the institutions and organizations of his community. He will accept or reject overtures to him and will himself make overtures to organizations insofar as he judges them currently most salient and also most feasible. Of course, since he cannot be certain of feasibility unless he gets inside a particular organization, this will imply the expenditure of some time and energy in exploration and trial efforts. At the start of a possible enterprise, a certain amount of educated guessing is inevitable; but the mark of the talented specialist is that he spends a minimum of time on fruitless explorations, and that he quickly makes up his mind to go forward when he judges all the complicated factors to be patterning auspiciously.

It was this type of thinking that impelled me to spend so much time talking with that young psychiatrist about his volunteer work and then building the relationship with the chairman of the diocesan planning committee. (See pp. 8 ff.) I believed that the church was currently highly salient from the point of view of community mental health; and the information I was receiving about its recent moves to organize a new program for parish clergy made me think that it might also rate high on feasibility. I therefore grasped the opportunity that chanced to present itself, and I willingly invested enough time and effort to explore the matter further. As soon as I discovered that my judgment seemed correct, I committed myself to whatever expenditure of resources might be needed to continue the collaborative process, in line with the model presented in this chapter.

The initial developments in our involvement with the United Methodist Church throw further light on these issues. This church is about three times the size of the Episcopal Church, and I imagine that it may therefore be even more salient than the latter as a caregiving agency that will affect the mental health of large numbers of people. At the present stage I have no way of knowing how high it rates on the scale of feasibility, i.e., how ready it may be to develop a mental health program in association with us or with the program of the Episcopalians, and how effective such a development may turn out to be. The amount of energy I am willing to devote to this project will depend on what transpires within the next few months, which may provide me with the necessary information for a judgment about its feasibility. It seems a positive sign that the Council of Bishops invited Bishop Richards to help them plan a support program for their new bishops. Perhaps this means that when a program has achieved a favorable reputation and has moved, as ours has, to a high level in one organization, it spreads to another organization at the highest level it has reached rather than at the bottom of the organizational structure. So although in the Episcopal Church we moved from parish clergy to diocesan bishop to House of Bishops Committee to Presiding Bishop, the process in the United Methodist Church may start at the very top. I hope that it will then filter down to the parish level because that is where the actions crucial for community mental health must take place. The danger of entering an organization at the top is that its executives may accept the structure of a program, but because of lack of firsthand experience may not have the detailed knowledge necessary to ensure an effective content; in our case that applies not only to mental health matters but also to the organizational supports needed at middle-management levels to master the expectable obstacles to implementation of the plans. It also includes the educated demand from line workers that something they value be organized or retained, as demonstrated in the recent developments in Massachusetts.

I trust that the present book will play a useful role in this connection. By its documentation of the detailed reality of the Massachusetts program at the parish level it may arouse the interest and the motivation of Methodist pastors, as well as line workers in other caregiving organizations, to initiate analogous programs of their own and eventually to ask their institutional leaders to provide the necessary organizational framework to foster these efforts.

In other words, although our model leads us to expect that on the basis of reputation we may move quickly from the local level to the top of an organization and then jump over to the top of a second organization, these considerations alert us to the need to follow up this rapid development by a long and careful process of working at intermediate and lower levels of

the organizations in order to ensure that the eventual programs have some solid substance and are not just made up of
slogans. In Ruth Caplan's earlier book,[2] she has amply docu-
mented how frequently this unfortunate process occurred during the development of mental health services in the United
States in the nineteenth century.

An important way of reducing this danger is to alert personnel at all levels of caregiving organizations as well as in community mental health agencies to the need for educating
themselves, both by theoretical studies and by practical experience linked with subsequent reflection, about the kind of issues raised in the present book, including the expectable organizational and human complications that will have to be
mastered in implementing an apparently simple plan for improving the mental health operations of a caregiving institution.

Timing and Styling of Intervention: Our model emphasizes
the importance of timing differentiated interventions into the
life of a caregiving agency. At each phase in the development
of our program in the Episcopal Church—and a similar picture is emerging with the United Methodist Church—a
characteristic process has been repeated. There has been an
initial interaction or series of interactions between the mental
health worker and representatives of the caregiving organization. This has been followed by a rather lengthy period of little
or no contact. This in turn has been succeeded by the relatively rapid appearance of a specific plan, which then leads to
a lengthy period of collaboration in implementing the plan.

Thus, after my first series of contacts with the young psychiatrist and the chairman of the planning committee, I heard
very little from the Episcopal Church in Massachusetts for
nearly two years, after which a diocesan program rapidly took
shape. Similarly, the Bishop-to-Bishop program developed
several months after the Philadelphia consultation meeting,

and during the intervening period I had little contact with the Pastoral Development Committee. A similar hiatus occurred for about a year between the participation of the two Methodist bishops in our second consultation training seminar and the invitation for Bishop Richards to offer consultation to the Council of Bishops.

In these instances it has eventually become clear that although contact with me was interrupted, the hiatus period represented a most important phase in the ongoing development. During that period key decision-makers in the other organization were engaged in an active process of integrating appropriate aspects of my ideas within their own thinking, working out a pattern of action that fitted the idiosyncratic needs and resources of their level of the organization, and soliciting support for their project from their peers and superiors. Only after they had made considerable progress with these tasks did they come back to me. In two instances, first, persuading Bishop Stokes to accept the suggestions of the Massachusetts planning committee that he be involved as a consultee in their program, and second, obtaining the Presiding Bishop's approval of the Bishop-to-Bishop program, I was asked to play a key role as part of the delegation seeking formal sanction. In a hierarchical organization it is obviously useful to bring in a high-status outsider when personnel negotiate with their superiors and feel the need for additional leverage. But, with these two exceptions, I was not asked to intervene in the intra-organizational tailoring and establishment of the programs I have described.

I believe that it is important for mental health specialists to recognize this hiatus phase, and not to try to push their way into something that is, and should remain, a private matter for the other organization. Despite our natural curiosity to find out how the process we have initiated is progressing and to evaluate whether we judged feasibility correctly or whether we have wasted our time, I feel that we should resist the temptation to take active steps during this period to discover what is happening inside the other organization. Such data collection will almost inevitably be interpreted by their staff as meddling in their private affairs and may spoil the smooth development of our relationship.

From these considerations it appears that the appropriate sequence of interventions by the mental health worker is as follows:

A. Initial activity in. responding to an inquiry through exploring the needs of the caregiving organization, describing what we have to offer that seems relevant to those needs, and expressing our willingness to work together insofar as it seems likely that while helping them we can achieve the goals of our own mission.

B. A hiatus period when we hold ourselves in readiness to respond, but initiate no action. Once we are called we should move immediately, because delay on our part may interfere with the internal timetable of the other organization.

C. Collaboration with the planners of the organization in shaping their plan and in negotiating sanction from their authority system, should the latter be requested.

D. Negotiation of the agreement for a joint effort that will satisfy the needs of both sides.

E. Implementing the plan by offering whatever service seems appropriate, such as education, individual and group consultation, collaboration in program planning and operation, or the like.

F. As soon as possible, the roles we play should be handed over to personnel of the caregiving organization, so that eventually we can move on to another organization and continue with our mission.

Importance of Intermediaries: By "intermediaries" I mean staff members or associates of the caregiving organization who act as communication bridges or mediators to inform us of its

needs and to transmit or translate our messages to their colleagues, active agents in developing or shaping the mental
health plan and promoting support for it inside their organization, and people who may take over our roles and perpetuate
them when we withdraw. As our case description so clearly
demonstrates, such intermediaries are an essential element in
the process envisaged in our model.

The psychiatric resident and the first and second chairman
of the planning committee played a crucial role in liaison between me and the Massachusetts Diocese; and subsequently
the chairman and the staff man at the diocesan headquarters
were largely responsible for establishing and maintaining our
diocesan program.

Equally obvious has been the importance of the part played
by Bishop Stokes and Bishop Richards in building a bridge
and maintaining communication between me and the Pastoral
Development Committee of the House of Bishops. But the out-
standing example of the crucial role of intermediary has been
the work of Bishop Richards in the Bishop-to-Bishop program.
Without him this program could never have been established.
He organizes the group of consultant bishops; he makes sure
that the Presiding Bishop's secretary sends a letter in good
time to all new bishops to invite them to choose a consultant;
he arranges the link-up between consultants and consultees;
he distributes descriptive material to all participants about the
reciprocal roles of consultants and consultees and about the
practical arrangements of consultation; he solicits consultation
reports; he organizes the supervisory group meetings; he re-
cruits new consultants and organizes my training seminars; he
offers guidance, support, and, whenever necessary, supervision
to the consultants; he invokes my help when it is needed; he
maintains communications with the Presiding Bishop and the
House of Bishops; he is building links between our program
and the United Methodist Church and is also exploring possible relationships with other churches; in short, he provides the

practical binding force that holds the entire program together. Without someone like him no countrywide program could ever be maintained for very long.

Bishop Richards is also beginning now to move into another role. For three years he has been participating in all my consultation seminars and supervisory sessions, and with my help he has begun to play an increasing role as an adviser on consultation technique to the bishop-consultants. In his recent meeting with the United Methodist Council of Bishops he was operating as a typical consultant, and on the previous day he and I discussed the practical issues that were likely to be involved. He was, in effect, replacing me on that occasion. It was interesting that the Methodists apparently felt more comfortable inviting him as their consultant than me, possibly believing that they would find it easier to discuss their organizational problems with a bishop, even from another church, than with a psychiatrist.

All this is moving in a most auspicious direction, and it looks as though in the not-too-distant future Bishop Richards may well feel able, and be perceived by others to be able, to take over most or all of my functions as a community mental health consultant to the Episcopal and other churches. I hope always to be available to assist him when he feels the need, but I imagine that eventually my time will be freed to move on to develop mental health endeavors in other caregiving organizations so that we may reach additional populations.

chapter 10

Support Systems

Gerald Caplan

Underlying much of what I have discussed in the previous chapter is a concept whose true significance we are just beginning to appreciate. This is the concept of "support systems." The idea that a person receives support or is in need of support usually carries the connotation that he is weak, and from this point of view the term is unfortunate, because what we have in mind is not the propping up of someone who is in danger of falling down but, rather, the augmenting of a person's strengths to facilitate his mastery of a stress or a challenge. The notion is rooted in our studies of the significance for mental health of a person's behavior during crisis, and it has recently been extended to cover also the supports that may help an individual or a group master chronic frustration or privation.

Crisis theory has been discussed by many community mental health workers. This is not the place for a detailed exposition of it;[1] but, briefly, the fundamental idea is that the manner in which an individual grapples with unexpected and temporarily insurmountable life problems that upset his customary mental equilibrium may have significant and lasting consequences for his future mental health. During the relatively short period of upset of each life crisis the individual is in danger of responding maladaptively, which will have a bad effect on him in the future; but he also has the opportunity to master the challenge in a way that will enhance his mental competence and maturity.

Our researches have demonstrated that a person's coping pattern during crises is very much influenced by the help or hindrance of other people, particularly friends and family, caregiving professionals, and peers or superiors at work. From this we have derived the idea of increasing the likelihood of positive mental health and reducing the risk of mental disorder in a population by improving the quality of interpersonal support that is provided to those in crisis by the significant people around them. And we are now beginning to analyze the nature of this support in order to discover what elements in it are most conducive to health promoting crisis mastery, and how such elements can best be organized so that they are provided in an acceptable form for people when and where they are needed.

My own understanding of these issues has been improved by analyzing the experience described in this book. Our program as a whole, as well as its parts, can be conceptualized as an organization of support systems. The parish clergyman is one of the significant community caregivers in offering help to individuals and families at crisis times. His traditional role prescribes systematic intervention in the lives of his parishioners during the developmental crises of marriage, birth, adolescence, and death; and he is readily available during the crises precipitated by accidental misfortunes such as illness, family disruptions, and loss of employment. People turn readily to him for counsel and support because they do not have to categorize themselves as "cases" in order to get his help.

But the parish clergyman himself also needs support, not only in dealing with the crises of sudden and unexpected professional demands but in maintaining his poise and freshness of spirit while being continually called upon to help his parishioners in their predicaments day after day, week after week, and month after month. His religion provides him with an important source of personal strength, and he passes some of this on to his parishioners while sharing its benefits with them in the mutual replenishment of religious services. Our experience over the past five years has, however, demonstrated to us that this is often not enough. Our consultation groups for parish clergy have helped to remedy a lack that many of them continually or intermittently feel.

In Chapter 8 Ruth Caplan discussed three types of help that clergymen derived from the consultation program: mental health knowledge and skills, peer support, and a reference group.

Have we, however, learned anything from our consultation program that can guide us in organizing some form of continuing support for those who no longer attend and also for those who for a variety of reasons do not come at all for consultation? I believe that the analysis of the three types of support provided by our groups does indicate some promising possibilities.

SUPPORTS FOR PARISH CLERGY

Mental Health Knowledge and Skills: First, the cognitive content about mental health, patterns of crisis-coping, methods of crisis intervention, and ways of assessing and managing cases of mental disturbance in parishioners and their families which is communicated by the psychiatric consultant through analysis of the weekly cases could be disseminated more widely, even if perhaps less effectively, by systematic continuation education courses and seminars. These could be taught by educators with less clinical qualifications and experience than our psychiatric consultants. Many psychologists and psychiatric social workers with educational talent could teach the material competently. The most appropriate educators would be clergymen with psychological training, since not only can they deal with the basic psychological and mental health topics but they can also speak authoritatively about the methods to be used by their profession in managing complicated cases.

Systematic continuing education that was regularly updated would provide parish clergy with knowledge and skills that they could call upon to deal more efficiently with many of the mental health problems they currently encounter, but we must expect that from time to time they will meet unusual cases that demand specialized handling. Our psychiatric consultants not only provide specific assistance to group members in such situations but guide them in building channels of communication and relationships to local mental health facilities which can provide the necessary specialist collaboration. For those ministers who are not able to get such help with exceptional cases from a consultation group led by a mental health clinician, it would be advisable for a diocese to organize a central or regional service to offer case-centered advice about assessment, disposition, referral, and, most important, linking with appropriate specialized agencies. When parish clergy can be helped to build enduring relationships with the staff of a nearby community mental health program, the problem of their being overburdened by exceptional cases will be much reduced.

This last suggestion may offer a way of replacing one other element in the supportive role of the psychiatrist in the consultation groups. Our psychiatric consultant is an authority to whom the group members can turn in an emergency and on whom they can rely for clarifying their confusions. I must confess that although I realize its importance, this is the aspect of our program that I like least because it tends to induce and perpetuate dependency in the consultees, even though our consultation techniques are carefully designed to counteract this. Nevertheless, in a less than perfect world we must face the fact that parish clergy, like the rest of us, will in conditions of stress tend to regress from their usual state of mature independence and will feel the need to rely on an authority figure. At least in our consultation program we are continually aware, while we satisfy this human need, of the danger of fostering undue dependency and of distorting the work style of members of another profession. How can we achieve similar results without using mental health consultants who are skilled in avoiding these hazards? I believe that the approach should be to provide within the diocesan or denomination structure authority figures who are clergymen with special competence in mental health matters and who have been trained to maintain as coordinate a relationship as possible with those who turn to them for help with a parish problem. Since the Episcopal Church is, in any case, a hierarchical system, it has developed a culture that guards against the dangers of undue dependency among its line workers; and if a parish clergyman should identify more than is ideal with his mental health authority figure, no great harm will follow because the mentor will be a member of his own profession and a bearer of the values and traditions of his own religion.

Peer Supports: Let us now turn to the second source of support in our consultation program, the peer group. This involves two major elements, the social-emotional supports of regular friendly interaction with those in the same boat who understand one's predicaments and share one's troubled feelings; and the help with tasks provided by those who describe how they have handled similar situations and what the consequences were. This part of our program seems the easiest to replace by analogues that can be reproduced on a wide scale throughout an area. All that is needed is to provide an opportunity for regular meetings of parish clergy in groups of appropriate size so that the correct intensity of relationship is likely to develop: if the groups are bigger than fifteen or twenty, people will not be able to get to know everyone and exclusionist cliques may form; if the group size falls below five or six, personal relationships may get too intense, which will not matter if they are positive, but which will splinter the group if they are negative or ambivalent.

Considering the obvious merits and simplicity of such a plan, it is interesting to me how difficult it has proved to implement. True, most dioceses, including Massachusetts, have one or more social and cultural clubs for their clergy, and they also intermittently organize district and regional meetings. The diocese also has a variety of standing and ad hoc committees and task forces that bring groups of clergymen together for regular encounters. But none of these seems to provide the right setting or atmosphere for obtaining the kind of consistent peer support in dealing with mental health problems of parishes and parishioners that is given by our consultation groups. The underlying obstacles need further study, but I believe that the crucial issue is a leadership problem. In order to foster optimally supportive relationships, both social-emotional and task-oriented, among a group of peers, the latter should not be competing for leadership of the group. Either the leader should be brought in from outside the organization, as in our program, or from another organizational level or area—for example, from the area administrator's office. If the "pecking order" in the group is quite clear and fixed, and if the group is otherwise culturally homogeneous, it might not upset matters if the leader were elected or appointed from its top-status layer; but the hierarchical nature of such a group would probably lead to an unbalanced pattern of supports, i.e., the lower-status members would get more support from the upper-status members than vice versa. The best pattern to foster peer support would be a group of equals, and in that case if the leader is not brought in from outside, rivalry might be reduced by allotting the leadership role to each member in rotation. This is, however, not likely to be satisfactory because not all are equally talented, and other members will attempt to make up for the deficiencies of the current leader by conscious or unconscious competition.

A related issue is that a coordinate group of peers who are

burdened by chronic professional or other stress have a hard time evaluating themselves and each other positively. Their interactions may easily take the form of pulling each other down rather than pulling each other up. Feelings of inferiority and failure in individuals can be unconsciously transferred to all or part of the group, and that often leads to a disintegrative process, probably a major reason why so many peer groups fall apart after a few meetings. It is the task of the leader to counteract this self-disparagement and to help the group members discover and build upon their strengths. If the leader is too close in formal status to the group members, he is apt to share their blind spots.

Whether or not these speculations of mine turn out to be validated by further study, I feel that the replacement of our consultation groups by other groups designed to foster organized peer support demands the organization of a cadre of "outside leaders." They do not have to be mental health clinicians, but they must be talented and experienced *chairmen* who know how to control group-destructive forces and maintain a group spirit that frees members to support each other along the lines I have previously discussed.

Another approach to the organization of such peer support is to legitimize and provide resources such as travel and modest entertainment allowances for parish clergy to build small informal friendship groups that meet regularly to chat about common work problems. Such friendship circles, in any case, develop spontaneously in all organizations. I am suggesting that a diocese might provide them with some measure of recognition and recommend to vestries and to parsons that absence from the parish for such interactions, however pleasurable they are, be treated as a potentially valuable job-related activity and not as a form of "goofing off."

Reference Groups: It must already be obvious that in my analysis of the topic of support systems I am continually striving to develop concepts that will provide models for programs that may have wider community impact because they make less use of psychiatrists in direct-action roles. My population-oriented philosophy calls for the community psychiatrist to start by getting firsthand knowledge of a problem area through diagnosing and treating emotionally disturbed individuals; then he should become a consultant and educator to enable other caregivers to handle such cases; later, he should consult with organizations so that they may develop policies and programs for the prevention and control of these disorders; and eventually he should hand over as many as possible of his consultation and educational functions to professionals and administrators of the caregiving organizations, so that he can free his own energy to repeat the entire sequence with some other segment of human troubles.[2]

From the point of view of this philosophy it would appear that my task of conceptualizing effective analogues to replace fundamental contributions of our mental health consultation groups is easiest in relation to the third type of supports that they offer. It is true that the inputs of the mental health consultant group leader are a factor in molding the values and traditions of the reference group in such matters as emphasizing the importance of a calm, methodical analysis of a confusing situation, avoidance of premature judgments because of frustration, and the belief that the most apparently inexplicable human behavior can be understood if we investigate enough intrasystemic and intersystemic connections among the phenomena of the case. But this whole style of methodical problem-solving and of testing the reality of perceptions and expectations in emotionally arousing work situations, which is the fundamental core of the ideology of the reference group, obviously also can be communicated by other influential people to the groups of clergymen. In fact, this ideology can probably be enunciated in more easily assimilable language and with greater affective power by opinion-molders within the church than by outsiders such as psychiatrists.

These considerations lead me to the conclusion that reference-group supports can be effectively organized by the bishop and his diocesan staff by communicating the requisite community mental health ideology through a variety of channels and vehicles and in many different settings, so that every clergyman will feel its impact in each contact he has with every other individual and group in the diocese. The goal must be the development of a diocese culture that prescribes normative behavior and ways of problem-solving in mental health matters with which all clergymen can identify unconsciously and thus feel free to behave in ways that come naturally to them when grappling with the human predicaments of their parish work. Their grasp of the shared ideology and their awareness of the certain approval of their peers and admired superiors when they operate in line with the dominant style of behavior provide them with a consonant internal and external set of supports that give them poise and self-confidence in making independent judgments and decisions, secure in the knowledge that they will be acting in the best traditions of their religious community. This is, of course, an idealized picture, but it clearly points the way for a bishop and his staff to turn their entire diocesan organization into a reference group that has immeasurably greater potency than that of a relatively peripheral program such as the one we mental health specialists have built in Massachusetts. Our place in such a larger endeavor would be to advise the bishop and his staff about content areas and methods of communication of the problem-solving style and not, as at present, to directly communicate the messages ourselves to occasional groups of consultees.

SUPPORTS FOR HEADS OF DENOMINATIONS

Bishops and other top denominational administrators need support just as much as parish clergy and parishioners, and for analogous reasons. The practical problem of providing them with appropriate supports is that, unlike ministers and parishioners, their peers and authority figures are distributed hundreds and thousands of miles apart, and personal contact with them is difficult and expensive to arrange. And yet the provision of effective support to them is particularly important because it is likely that an adequately supported top administrator will more consistently fulfill the needs for supports of his parish clergy, who will in turn be better able to satisfy the needs of their parishioners. This was the rationale for the demand by the Massachusetts planning committee composed of parish clergy that their bishop receive consultation as an essential element in their proposed program for parsons.

The same three basic elements of support systems apply to bishops as they do to parish clergy and parishioners. The bishops need knowledge and skills—in their case about how to set up a supportive structure in the diocese along the lines we have just discussed. They need authority figures to whom they can turn for occasional guidance and support in especially difficult diocesan predicaments. They need peer support, both social-emotional and task-oriented; they get some of this from meetings of the House of Bishops and its committees, but not enough. They need a reference group to be the bearer and communicator of a productive mental health ideology—again the House of Bishops should be the answer, but this body serves many functions and it probably should establish a specialized unit to achieve this special goal.

Some, but not all, of the elements of such supports can be provided by a mental health specialist through individual consultation; and wherever skilled mental health consultants are available, bishops would be well advised to invoke their assistance, as have Bishop Stokes and Bishop Burgess in Massachusetts. Since the number of bishops in the country is relatively small, this will not overtax our specialist resources; the only obstacle is that in some areas skilled mental health consultants may not be available.

In addition, the Bishop-to-Bishop program provides a service that offers not only the benefits of mental health-style consultation but also peer support, and, through the medium of the group of consultant-bishops which meets regularly for training and supervisory sessions, the beginnings of a reference group. At present this reference group caters mainly to the consultants. It is conceivable that in the future the consultees may have a group of their own, and in any case after they have themselves received consultation for two years many of them will probably graduate into the ranks of the consultants and join that reference group. If the program continues and is successful, it will after a few years have involved the majority of members of the House of Bishops either as consultants or as consultees or both, and by that time the House of Bishops itself will have become the bearer of the reference-group mental health ideology.

All that remains in order to complete the logic of this pattern is to organize a support system for the Presiding Bishop, and I hope that this eventually will be accomplished.

I will conclude my presentation by pointing out that this program promises the achievement of the ultimate goal of our population-oriented philosophy. I am now in the process of transmitting to the leaders of the caregiving organization the skills that my profession has developed. The bishops have learned these skills and are, with my help, adapting them to their own particular setting. In the not-too-distant future, Bishop Richards probably will take over my remaining training and supervisory roles, and I will move on, leaving in operation a countrywide, self-perpetuating support system that should ensure the fostering of analogous supports in all the dioceses and in all the parishes of the Episcopal Church. This, at least, is the grand design. I believe we have a good chance of achieving our goals, and all the predictive indications are currently auspicious. I hope that this development may continue.

chapter 11

Consultation: The View from Headquarters

Anson Phelps Stokes, Jr.

The value of the mental health consultation program described in this book must ultimately be judged by the well-being of the people, out in the communities, who have been helped by their clergy. This will take a long time to assess and many factors will have to be considered. If, however, it is hard to measure the benefit to the "helped," it is quite easy to recognize the benefit to the "helpers."

Clergy who have participated in the program have referred to it as a "life-saver." For it has helped them in a crucial area of the ministry, which affects the esteem in which they are held and their own self-confidence in their profession.

A minister may be a good preacher, an able parish administrator and leader in his community—but if he fails to help people who turn to him with their problems, he fails at a point which deeply affects his spirit and his work. Likewise, if he helps people with their problems, he is likely to be a better preacher and to have a better understanding of the purpose of parish life and his role in the parish and community. Clergy who have benefited from this program have been relieved from overburdening anxieties and become better clergy. Also their relationship to the diocese is likely to be more positive because they recognize and appreciate its function in supporting them.

204

Thus consultation becomes a factor in the well-being of people, parishes, and the diocese.

No discussion of the merits of our program would be complete, however, without some description of its benefits to me personally as the chief executive, in facing the administrative and pastoral problems of diocesan leadership. I will frequently use the term "chief executive" because I know that my role as bishop has many counterparts in other denominations and that all of us can profit from consultation. Our roles may be understood in various terms, yet all of us consider ourselves more than administrators. We have spiritual and pastoral responsibilities and opportunities for community leadership and service. We need consultation as much as our clergy do. A mark of this particular program is that it helped "headquarters" as well as the parishes.

Only recently did I know that it was the clergy who insisted that I be involved as well as they. No doubt they recognized my own need, in dealing with them, of the support and skills that the program could offer. Quite likely they felt more prepared to commit themselves to consultation if I were to be "in it" along with them. I suspect that, in addition to these reasons, they were conscious that we live in a time when questions of structure and administration are being rethought and that the role of the diocese and its leader needed to be reexamined with the best help available.

To put it briefly and with some oversimplification: I started as executive of the diocese in 1956, when there seemed to be many pressures calling for centralized leadership and I closed my episcopate at the end of 1969, when there seemed to be a strong desire for decentralization and local initiative. There are obviously many factors involved in this change. They include finances, personalities, social problems, population movements, and changing styles of work. At the beginning there were some who wanted decentralization and at the end there were a few who wanted central leadership. By and large, however, the above-mentioned change toward decentralization was clear. No doubt there will always be changes in the concept of leadership desired and no one pattern will continue forever. Consultation will be needed "at headquarters" as well as "in the field."

CHURCH EXTENSION

The period of the late fifties and early sixties was a time of church expansion. There was talk of a "return to religion." Churches grew numerically as people moved and new suburbs were developed. To keep pace with these pressures the churches, nationally and locally, developed structures for extension. In different denominations it was handled in different ways. Some had national offices which offered expertise in terms of surveys, financial resources—or guidance in raising them—and even in architectural planning and construction. The Episcopal Church looked to its local dioceses for the major responsibility in these matters. Much of my early days was involved in planning, surveys, consultation with interchurch bodies (for we were beginning to see dangers in competition), and in encouraging strategic growth. We appointed, and helped to support, missionary clergy, and had on our diocesan staff three archdeacons who spent a large measure of their time starting and guiding new and growing churches. The diocese was looked to for funds, architectural assistance, and general strategy. We launched in 1964 a major Diocesan Advance Fund campaign, largely for funds for grants and loans for new and growing work. This was an exciting and successful undertaking. It followed a diocesan survey, contracted for from our national headquarters, which had pointed up needs in many geographical areas.

To be sure, all was not roses. We began to notice the decline of traditional church life in urban parishes and our Archdeacon of Boston (who subsequently became my successor as bishop of the diocese) kept reminding us of the need for new strategies and funds for the inner city—but in this area too it was felt that financial and other leadership from "headquarters" was indicated.

However, we were also beginning to turn our concern more and more to a rethinking of our basic goals. An English bishop, to whom I spoke with pride about our very successful capital-funds drive, was not overly impressed! "We are beginning to think," he said, "that in these days the church must travel light." Once again the national church body gave leadership in promoting study conferences that raised these deeper issues. We came more and more to question our overhead structure and expansionist ideas, and readier to rethink the mission of the Church to an urbanized and decaying society where race and poverty played determining roles. The question was no longer "Where shall we put new churches?" We had to consider what church life itself was intended to be. The "return to religion" soon proved superficial. Most of the pressing needs for new churches were eventually met. We then faced the desperate needs in the inner city—from which those who now supported growing churches had fled. Eventually capital funds for grants were expended. Rotating loan funds were slow in being repaid. New types of need were becoming obvious. "Bricks and mortar" began to take second place.

CHRISTIAN EDUCATION

As World War II ended there was a general recognition of the almost complete failure of Sunday schools. Indeed, this concern had increased even in the face of church expansion. Once again "headquarters" gave leadership and our church, nationally, following on the heels of the Presbyterians, developed a new curriculum. It began with adult education and study of the Faith. When I became bishop the newly developed Seabury Series curriculum was aimed at the very heart of our church life—for the leaders had made a discovery. The giving of information, alone, whether biblical or ecclesiastical, was often not only unsuccessful but also irrelevant to the real-life situations of our children and adults. We were answering questions that they had not asked. We had failed to start where they were and to involve them in real religious experience or commitment. The new curriculum concerned itself with the "process" of religious development as well as with the "content" of the Faith (some felt it did not give enough content—church enthusiasms often swing far in one direction and then in another). The burgeoning interest in group dynamics was tapped for use by the church. The parish is a "group," and we were helped to understand how groups act and how we learn through them. Clergy and laity quickly learned the meaning of "hidden agenda," "feedback," "training" (or "T" groups), "consensus," etc. They gained new techniques, like "role-playing" and other methods of eliciting response. Parish Life Conferences were set up which helped people to think through their own parish's life. This had a spiritual dimension. Many gained a new understanding of forgiveness through their "acceptance" by their peers. The movement had many dangers—but it had a potential safeguard. Unlike some secular groups, the church had something positive to give people when they were ready for it. The Gospel often became relevant in group experience. People need not be "opened up" and left without resources. Starting with their needs, the Gospel could speak to them effectively.

The movement carried on leadership-training groups at varying levels, and it continues today. It has many dangers when regarded as a cure-all or when led by unwise leaders. Some individuals have gone overboard, so to speak. However, it has deeply influenced our church life with new insights and new techniques.

At first one of my clearly conceived tasks was to encourage the use of the Seabury Series and help to foster the deeper group life of the parish that went with it. About one-third of our parishes in the diocese adopted the Series, but at least another third was influenced by it, and new vigor and personal commitment were fed into the bloodstream of these parishes. The church was being understood more as a community than as an institution.

However, once again the role of centralized leadership was seen to have certain problems. The very efforts of departments and executives to set up this program contradicted the flexibility and human understanding which the new approach sought to emphasize. Indeed, in wrong hands, group dynamics could be an instrument of manipulation. Much of its ideology was accepted, but those who accepted it then no longer wanted to be "sold" anything! They wanted help on their terms and in their particular needs.

In 1966 a carefully planned diocesanwide adult-education effort had been launched, called the Diocesan Venture in Faith. It followed after the financial effort of the Diocesan Advance Fund. Like that, it developed a wide participation and a sense of diocesan unity. But this united diocesanwide effort could not go on indefinitely. Local people wanted local programs tailored to their situations. In the past few years the services of Christian Education specialists have become a resource to be called upon, rather than a program to be promoted.

SOCIAL ACTION

A third area in which this process of centralization and decentralization was revealed was in that of social concern. The diocese had a long history of action for prison reform, planned parenthood, opposition to the death penalty, etc. After World War II over two thousand refugees, from war-torn or communist-dominated lands, had been resettled. A strong Department of Christian Social Relations guided the parishes, encouraging them to sponsor refugee families, helping them to provide hospitality and to find housing and employment. There was also concern for the aging and for youth and others facing particular problems. Quite a lot of direct social service was carried on by headquarters staff.

As the civil-rights movement grew, much was done to support churchmen who went south to share in demonstrations. A series of area conferences in the diocese were set up on Race. These were carefully planned so that whites were—sometimes for the first time—confronted by the attitudes of blacks, and faced the realities of black feelings and of their own prejudices. The bishop was called upon to back up Boston Negroes in a school strike for better urban schools, and to assist poor people demonstrating for decent housing. The Vietnam War led many clergy and laity to activist expressions of concern. In the area of industry, the diocese sponsored conferences on Christianity and Business, in which the ethical responsibilities of church people were explored using cases to bring out the issues. We helped set up an ecumenical Boston Industrial Mission, which used the expertise of research and development people to face social issues. The value of having church leaders who could speak for the church was apparent. Diocesan conventions and interdenominational assemblies expressed themselves in resolutions on many issues.

These centralized efforts were extremely helpful. Yet once again they were followed by a desire for emphasis on local action by local churches, using local resources and often working interdenominationally. A diocesanwide "Diocesan Call to Action" found itself moving from centralized programs to the encouragement of local initiative. The diocese was no less concerned now than it was in the past, but its services were changing in method. Indeed the "street ministries" it now supports under my successor are served by men who work in the field, and exist primarily to respond to local calls for help. The office role is minimized.

Typical was our experience in racial matters. At one time

the diocese supported a black priest who was my adviser in racial matters. Then we helped to develop an ecumenical Commission on Race in the Massachusetts Council of Churches and made it possible for the black minister to work for that commission. Finally, this ecumenical effort gave way to a Black Ecumenical Commission. We contributed to its support, but its initiatives were entirely with the black community. Sometimes, rather than work specifically through a religious organization, our finances were used to help effective secular movements. Grants without strings were made to appropriate community organizations working for racial justice, inner city education, or good housing. Our national church was doing the same on a national level and we contributed to its efforts.

I have mentioned these particular ventures to point out that the complex leadership-role of a bishop, or other chief executive, was changing. Let me mention two general concerns which increasingly had an impact on that role: the church's structure and concern for the clergy.

STRUCTURE

People who were facing the issues I have mentioned found themselves questioning the church's structure and its adaptability to these developing functions.

Much of our investment in land and buildings seemed to hold the church back from flexibility precisely at a time of population movement and tremendous new human needs. Many questioned traditional church organizations which often sought to "hold people close to the church" rather than to "send them out" to serve the World.

We asked ourselves whether we were challenging our best lay talent. Were we giving them "Mickey Mouse" duties? Did our liturgy relate to life? How could we be prophetic and effective in facing evil in the world? Were diocesan affairs dominated by a small in-group of clergy and laymen? Could we broaden the base of participation at both parish and diocesan levels to include a wider cross section sociologically and geographically and including youth and minorities? How could we support clergy who took bold stands on controversial issues and, at the same time, how could we prevent unnecessary polarization? How could parishes be led to take a good look at themselves and determine needs and opportunities, and plan accordingly? How could we experiment with new forms of worship and new emphases without unnecessarily hurting loyal people who were sustained in a time of change by old and familiar ways? How could we sort out the valid in new ideas and yet not follow every fad? How could the church be "spiritual" and at the same time relevant to social issues?

All these things affected the structures of the diocese and the role of the bishop as its leader. Diocesan departments came to be regarded as too rigid, and task forces began to take their place. The latter could do a job and then go out of business. Nationally, there was a concern for the planning process, and training in it was offered. Locally, staff members were encouraged to work for and with people in the field. Communication became a great concern. In 1961–62 we had a management survey dealing with our central structure. This study was helpful in its time—but it preceded the day of decentralization, flexibility, "de-departmentalizing," and financial stringency. Our administrative structures needed overhauling anew.

CONCERN FOR THE CLERGY

As we faced needed changes in structure, the human units involved became more, not less, important and there was a growing concern about the well-being of the clergy. For years, questions of salary, housing, medical insurance, and retirement had been with us. Steps had been taken—but not enough. Now the clergy were, in many instances, raising deeper considerations. Dedicated to service, they recognized their need for more than material support. They craved opportunities to improve their skills and to be renewed by continuing education. Their needs in this line led, as we have seen, via convention action, to our adopting the program with the Laboratory of Community Psychiatry. They also wanted counsel and career evaluation and a fairer, less haphazard, placement process. It is significant that, nationally, steps have recently been taken in all these areas in most denominations— including the Episcopal Church. These steps have involved national and diocesan planning, but a planning that takes its guidance from the expressed needs of those who will benefit from it. In some dioceses, clerical "unions" are pressing for change. They want clear-cut "contracts" between ministers and congregations specifying parish goals, job descriptions, and opportunities for continued study.

All the new structural and institutional aids that are developed will not minimize pastoral pressures on bishops or other executives. We will have the added task of working imaginatively to help our people discover, evaluate, and guide whatever new structures are indicated, and we will still be responsible to meet expressed or unexpressed needs for help.

Nowhere is help more needed than in our pastoral ministry to our clergy. When a pastoral crisis arises, ministers are expected to drop everything to work with it, and they in turn want leaders sufficiently unencumbered to drop everything also and help them. However (because we cannot always drop everything), other resources must be made available also. Frequently clergy can most effectively help each other if only local opportunities for knowing each other can be developed. This has been one by-product of the consultation groups.

In this changing setting, I found consultation with Dr. Gerald Caplan a "life-saver" in my work as bishop. Let me describe it from my point of view.

The word "bishop" has many role implications and I discovered that my peers in other churches found themselves facing many similar implications in their roles.

Traditionally we are leaders who represent and administer the church in a given area. Even in the least hierarchical denominations, this implies spiritual leadership. We are called to help set the "tone" of the church in our area. Some of us have responsibility for selecting and guiding seminarians and for ordaining the ministers. In one way or another we help in their placement and we must develop support systems for them after they are placed. Some of us have real administrative authority and can move clergy. We Episcopalians have little authority but some influence in their placement. We are called upon to be preachers and teachers. Most of us have responsibilities vis-à-vis our national church and we are often the links between it and our own area. We are symbols of the Church's unity in space, and some of us claim to represent its continuity in history also. Most of us have interdenominational duties and are called upon to help secular movements of various kinds. For all these tasks, most of us have had no special training beyond seminary and the parish ministry.

As no one executive can fulfill equally all these roles, we are torn in many directions. My consultations with Dr. Caplan started out, as he has already described, with the task of helping him to understand my church and my work. If I were to summarize the chief value of consultation to me, it was in helping me to understand my role.

One instance I remember clearly. I was facing a sticky problem in which a clergyman was at odds with his parish. Consultation led me not only to reduce my anxiety level and to evaluate the problem, but also to realize just how much authority I had to force some action. Pastoral relationships are helped, and not hurt, if one enters them with a clear-cut understanding of what authority one can and cannot exert. One then works within definite parameters. Not only the fact that Dr. Caplan always came to my office to see me in my setting and learn a lot about my work, but the fact that he practiced his religion made him sensitive to my spiritual responsibilities. On at least one occasion he pointed out that a problem I was facing was not psychological but moral. A psychiatrist who holds you up to your moral responsibility is impressive and helpful!

Dr. Caplan once quoted to me the result of a survey of necessary skills in management, made by a university group at considerable expense. It resulted in the recognition that the chief quality required in an administrator was the requirement that he "be himself." I soon found in the consultation process that one cannot change oneself completely. Every man has to be true to his own style. He must, however, be aware of its limitations, as well as of its strengths. I believe that one of Dr. Caplan's chief values to me was his apparent recognition of the validity of my style. He upheld me in my own role-image—strengthening it in many instances and indirectly helping me to modify it in others. The stress, however, was never on any abstract image, but on the requirements of the particular administrative and pastoral "cases" I brought to him.

I realize that the fact that he was a Jew, to whom I was trying to explain my situation objectively, was an added help in making me describe things I might otherwise take for granted. However, I believe that a similar consultant relationship can be developed between fellow professionals, e.g., between two church executives. It would require that the consultant have good sense and some training in consultation. Indeed, it might save time, as the consultant would already be familiar with the tasks of the consultee. The experience with Bishop-to-Bishop consultation bears me out.

ISSUES AT HEADQUARTERS

Dr. Caplan has mentioned most of the problem areas of my own work covered in my consultations with him. I can only add a few comments as to the values I found in facing various specific tasks.

The relationships between diocesan staff members and myself, and their relationships to each other and to their tasks, were often discussed. Consultation helped me to see the issues involved more clearly. There were always the personal needs, special concerns and individual styles of the staff members which had to be recognized and, when possible, fulfilled. Yet there were also the objective tasks for the common good which it was my duty to assign and lead them to carry out.

I was particularly pleased by the attitude of the staff toward my consultations. I spoke openly and enthusiastically about the program and, instead of being threatened by it, the staff seemed to approve it and to like what it was doing for their "boss." Dr. Caplan came to be held by them in high regard. Often staff members would raise questions with me which they hoped I would discuss with him. When they were occasionally present they were helped by him in the same ways that I was helped. In one case after being present at one of our consultations, a staff member set up meetings with other staff members to clarify his relationships with them.

The planning of diocesan conventions has been mentioned. Here the issue seemed to be the need for getting things done expeditiously, on the one hand, and the need for plenty of opportunity for grass-roots discussion, on the other. Both goals had their advocates among clergy and laymen. However, as time went on, the desire for wider participation increased and we found ways of giving more people time to contribute their ideas—without interfering with the dispatch of business. This has, since my retirement, been assisted by the fuller development of district meetings, of clergy and lay delegates, to which have been assigned definite responsibilities in developing diocesan policy.

In facing clergy/parish conflicts, I was helped to weigh my responsibility for the welfare of the clergy, on the one hand, and my responsibility for the welfare of the parishes, on the other. Needless to say, I had to be concerned about both. In consultation my anxiety level was reduced and I saw both personal and organizational issues more clearly. When conflicts arose my consultant helped me to see the courses of action available to me—canonically as well as pastorally! His own experience, both as a clinician dealing with individuals and as a consultant to organizations, was extremely valuable.

The personal and family problems of individual clergy were often under consideration. Occasionally, when a critical situation required psychiatric help, he would refer me to an available resource. (The consultants to the clergy groups did likewise.) Nearly always, however, he emphasized the adequacy of my own profession—if rightly exercised. At headquarters, as well as in the field, ministers were expected to be ministers and not to try to become psychiatrists.

Indeed, my consultant often pointed to the therapeutic value of much that is traditional in church life—and sometimes neglected. He once cited a study of widowhood in a certain area of Boston, made by the Laboratory of Community Psychiatry. It revealed the need for the old-fashioned pastoral calls made by clergy in their parishioners' homes. The fifty-minute counseling sessions given by ministers in their studies are not an adequate substitute for pastoral calls. A great reward of consultation has been the recognition of our spiritual roles—at headquarters and in the parishes.

My own view from headquarters has been reinforced since I have retired by my experience as a consultant in the Bishop-to-Bishop program now launched on a national basis. I have been impressed with the welcome extended by practically all bishops to whom consultation has been offered. Both of my consultees live far from Massachusetts, in areas with supposedly different points of view. On my first consultation visit, I feared that I would be suspect as a meddling member of the Eastern Establishment. Instead, I found that I was welcomed warmly by my consultee, who had discussed the planned relationship with his lay and clerical leaders. They too were delighted with the plan and very appreciative of the national church for providing such a resource for their bishop. From the very start, he felt free to share his problems. There is every evidence that this will be a growing movement, because it meets needs. It cannot be forced, but I believe that it will be widely used because it is so very adaptable to different situations.

As more and more church executives are helped by similar programs, I trust that they, in turn, can set up adaptations of them for the ministers in their jurisdictions (though it may, as with us, start at the grass roots). It may be difficult to find consultants like Dr. Caplan and the Fellows at the Laboratory of Community Psychiatry. But I believe that their concerns are spreading in the mental health field, and I know that skills in consultation can be learned. Former Fellows, who have shared in this program here, are now working in many parts of the country and may be available for similar programs in other areas.

At a recent training meeting for bishop-consultants, we celebrated Holy Communion in the same hotel room in which we shared experiences and problems. It was a simple and meaningful service. As I looked around the group of some seventeen fellow bishops, I felt a deep unity between our basic Christian commitment and the consultation program in which we were engaged. This program is both an extension of our basic vocation and a timely support of it. It is providentially suited to our need of support. It can help make the Church more effective in serving the basic needs of God's children.

chapter 12

Implications for the Church

David E. Richards

The term "pastoral development" refers to the elaboration, reenforcement, and refinement of systems, methods and techniques for providing effective pastoral care. It assumes that in any pattern of pastoral care the needs of the caregivers cannot be ignored without seriously curtailing the effectiveness of the system. The term has meaning only when the word "pastoral" is interpreted to include concern both for those who are ill or very deeply troubled and for those who currently enjoy health and reasonable stability but at the same time desire growth and the ever fuller realization of their own potential. Pastoral development is both curative and preventative: its goals include both healing from illness and self-actualization.

Dr. Caplan and Bishop Stokes, in their respective chapters, have both pointed out some implications for the church and its pastoral ministry to be found in mental health consultation for clergymen. In this chapter we wish to underscore several points already raised and to elaborate on the need and place of mental health consultation as an important development and implementation of the church's pastoral ministry. We shall do this by discussing separately the two distinct forms of mental health consultation for clergymen which have developed—namely, the coordinate-status form for church administrators and the task-oriented form for parish clergy. After we have examined the implications of this development for pastoral ministry, we shall briefly survey certain approaches other than mental health consultation that have proven to be resources for pastoral development.

THE COORDINATE-STATUS
FORM OF CONSULTATION

In the past decade, as Bishop Stokes' chapter already shows, church administrators have faced a number of new problems, some pertaining to the rapid changes in society, others to the church's own organization and the welfare of the clergy. In this last category, for example, there has been an increase in the number of resignations from the active ministry, and a growing trend toward voluntary, non-stipendiary ministry. Most recently, there has developed a shortage of openings and an over-supply of personnel for the clerical placements available. The situation has been aggravated by spiraling inflationary costs leaving less funds available to churches so that if clergymen are to receive adequate salaries, fewer will have to be employed. The church administrator has had to face such questions as church responsibility toward those who cannot find placement, the limits that must be placed on the recruitment of young men to the ministry, and how to deploy personnel when financial means are severely restricted.

These and other current problems are very difficult to solve, yet the church administrator is expected to find near-perfect answers to them. His quality of leadership is expected to be faultless and consistently masterful, although his resources for finding correct answers and for supplying dynamic leadership are generally thought to be invisible. It has been only very recently, and then in a limited way, that there has begun a realistic assessment of the needs of church executives. It is now recognized that whether he be a bishop, archbishop, district superintendent, executive secretary, stated clerk, or council president, the church administrator is subject to all the hazards of executive loneliness and, therefore, in need of a workable support system.

In church bodies which have gone through some form of analysis and restructuring, notice has usually been taken of the needs of the chief executive and provision made in the altered structure for some form of support system. However, this modification in structure is accomplished only with great effort and sometimes great expense. The process is slow and, in certain larger churches, takes a very long time to come about.

One of the great advantages of the coordinate-status consultation explained by Dr. Gerald Caplan is that it can begin immediately and church administrators do not need to wait until the entire administration and organizational structure of the church is overhauled. The adoption of coordinate-status consultation goes swiftly to the heart of the problem. From the very outset it deals effectively with the executive's isolation and opens up for him channels of communication which are beneficial and humanizing.

Coordinate-status consultation is especially needed today because change in many vital areas is forcing upon religious bodies and their chief administrators a host of new decisions and new requirements. The speed of change is such that even the most skillful reorganization may be out of date by the time it is effected and put into practice. Recently I was personally involved in the restructuring of a national church organization. Extensive care and thought went into an elaborate plan for reform and restructure. Just as the blueprint was completed, the drastic economic crunch which afflicted numerous voluntary organizations in 1969 and 1970, occurred; a massive staff reduction took place, and the entire restructuring was abandoned. There was no time to deal with the support needs of a number of key executives. The human damage and suffering that resulted cannot be measured. My point is that in church organizations we cannot afford to make the genuine, personal, and professional needs of executives dependent upon the restructuring of the organization. Coordinate-status consultation is a feasible and inexpensive way of supplying, without structural reorganization, a support system of which executives are the beneficiaries. And because they are benefited, many others in the system receive benefit and support that would not otherwise be available.

There is another significant advantage to be found in coordinate-status consultation: while the newly appointed or elected church executive is receiving some help or support as he tackles a job for which he has probably had no specific orientation or training, he is also learning a skill. As a consultee and the recipient of assistance from a more experienced executive, he is also learning how to be a consultant. This skill he can put to work immediately in the execution of his own task and later employ fruitfully when he assumes the consultant's role in a coordinate-status consultation. At present in the Episcopal Church, for example, we have had to initiate our consultant-training program among bishops lacking the experience of having been consultees. Within five or ten years, however, all the bishops in the program should have had experience in a consultee role. Out of their richer experience they will have perceptions and insights that we cannot now supply quite so well to those whom we are presently training as consultants. Learning how to make use of a consultation service and learning how to provide effective consultation are both ways of enriching the church administrator's work experience and adding to the wisdom and good judgment with which the administrative task is performed.

THE TASK-ORIENTED FORM OF CONSULTATION

A significant number of clergymen are today experiencing loss of meaning in their work and in their role-fulfillment.

Some have been victimized by institutional survival goals which have caused clergy as a professional group to be overworked and underpaid. A good deal of the overwork syndrome to be found among ministers can be traced to their not feeling competent in certain areas of their professional work; as a consequence, they have assuaged their guilt by putting in long hours on less complex tasks which become increasingly unrewarding and meaningless. This burdensome workload can be displaced only when a minister learns how to function professionally and to be creatively selective in choosing those tasks which are genuinely appropriate to his office.

Sometime ago I placed a call to a parish clergyman in a distant city and was told by the custodian of the building that he had just stepped down the street to purchase some light bulbs. I was annoyed not because it was inconvenient to be unable to reach him at that time, but because it appeared that for some strange reason he was doing the custodian's work. (This kind of errand, of course, can be very serviceable in an emergency.) However, in the case of a clergyman, it is damaging because it siphons off time and energy that should be used to bring light where it is desperately needed—namely, to the hearts and minds and souls of persons who need light by which to recover their health or to grow up to their next level of development.

A clergyman chooses to run such errands when he is uncertain about how to foster growth among his congregants. He runs such errands to avoid dealing with his own need for light and growth. Of the one thing we can be certain: when he chooses to run errands, purchase supplies, do clerk-typist work or perform bookkeeping functions, he may be contributing to institutional survival, but he is utterly wasting his time as a highly trained church professional with a valuable and needed function to perform in his community.

In recent years there have been many surveys and reports on clergy needs and morale. Out of these studies came a variety of suggestions for dealing with some of the problem areas. Clergy associations of different types, for example, were formed in certain areas. Some of these associations resembled local trade unions and clamored for the opportunity to "negotiate" salaries, housing, placement, etc. Others assumed a more dignified guise and resembled county medical associations with an emphasis on professional development, claiming that their goal was to upgrade their members professionally. Programs for continuing education began to receive more attention, and attempts were made to clarify the role of the minister.

In the forefront of these developments was a preoccupation with questions of professional identity: What function does a clergyman serve? By what criteria do congregations measure their need for institutional, full-time, paid professional ministers? By what standards do they measure the effectiveness of ordained personnel? What is the clergyman's real task, and does the congregation share this understanding?

Simultaneously, among the clergy, various fears become manifest: the fear of unemployment; the fear of never attaining "advancement"; the fear of being "stuck" in the same place; and the fear of having to seek secular employment. The emergence of such fears in various forms complicated the whole question of professional identity.

Even the most enlightened screening, selection, and pre-ordination training cannot be related to this segment of a person's experience. It must be noted that this experience occurs after the clergyman has achieved his early role-identification —that is, after he has completed the pre-ordination screening-selection-training process—and that theological schools do not have the resources to prepare him adequately for facing this kind of problem. The successful management of the problem, then, will depend on whether the structure of the religious institution includes the kind of support system to assist him toward a continuing definition of his identity and in facing what may prove to be a painful and, perhaps, costly readjustment.

Professional identity is achieved essentially in terms of competently fulfilled responsibilities. The basic issue for the average clergyman is deciding in just what areas of his multi-faceted role he is secure. The great enemy of identity is a low self-image and self-doubt. When one knows what he can do and when he is reasonably certain that he can do it well, then he has a good hold on his identity and will not be threatened by crises and hardship. On the other hand, when a clergyman does not see his function clearly and when he is fuzzy in his own mind about how well he performs his task, then the soil is just right for a harvest of doubt, uncertainty, continuing mediocrity, chronic depression, long-term unhappiness—in short, for a loss of identity.

The kind of learning to be found in task-oriented consultation is both an instrument of education and a means of affirming one's identity. It focuses on skill development in the area that traditionally has always belonged to the minister of religion as a caregiver. It can affirm pastoral identity by enhancing the functioning of the clergyman as he ministers in at least three ways to the spiritual and emotional health of his people.

First, the parish or congregational minister usually functions in the roles of teacher and preacher. Regularly he talks to people in small groups and larger groups about the meaning of life. Much of what he has to say is related to value systems, ethical behavior, and interpersonal relationships. His public ministry, therefore, upholds certain standards; and he is fortunate and unique among professionals in that along with being a practitioner in his special field (i.e. pastoral care), he is also a public lecturer and teacher of principles that contribute to the spiritual, emotional, and physical health of his clientele. His deeper understanding of his pastoral opportunities and his clinical experience in ministering to his congregants will enrich his preaching and teaching and add depth and meaning to his public ministry.

Secondly, in his role as pastoral visitor to the homes and places of work of his congregants, he has magnificent opportunities daily to relieve social isolation and to express warm and genuine concern for persons in need. Sometimes the needs to which he ministers in this way are agonizingly chronic. There is little observable improvement and the pain goes on throbbing month after month—even year after year. Some pastors weary of routine visiting because it does not seem to change situations noticeably or to accomplish any institutional goals; indeed, when it is not done, life seems to go on all the same. So why not take out an hour or a day or a month to purchase light bulbs or run assorted errands which at least produce some tangible result?

To understand the purpose and the value of pastoral visitation and to know how to give each visit increased meaning requires a kind of perception and sensitivity which cannot be taught in divinity school. They are insights that must emerge in the practice itself of pastoral care. The clinical understanding and critical evaluation of pastoral visiting acquired in task-oriented consultation will sharpen the pastor's sensitivity and save parish visiting from being dull, fruitless, and boring.

Thirdly, it is generally accepted by congregations and communities that in certain crisis situations the minister has a specific role to play. Meetings can be missed and social engagements broken with impunity if the clergyman is called to be present at a time of death, accident, or critical illness. He is expected to respond *swiftly*, but in order to respond *skillfully* he may need continuing training and the continuing refinement of his skills as a crisis interventionist.

The management of crisis has begun to be an area of special study in itself. Research and investigation have identified the principles to follow in crisis intervention. Certain myths pertaining to crisis have been exploded. It has been discovered that while a crisis is an event of considerable disorder, this very disorder follows a distinguishable pattern. Different stages can be identified, and different actions and initiatives are appropriate at different stages. To my knowledge theological schools

do not yet normally offer courses on crisis intervention, and yet
it is inevitable that every parish clergyman will have his share
of crisis calls. Exchange about these experiences with his peers
and in consultation with a behavioral scientist will help the
clergyman learn more and more about the dynamics of crisis
and his own responses to different types of crisis.

Over the centuries ministers, priests, and rabbis fulfilled a
mental health role in society long before the term itself was in-
vented. When mental health became a recognized specialty,
the role of the clergyman, at least in some minds, became confused, and some clergymen undertook to become specialists.
However, it seems to me that today we are becoming free of
that early confusion. We now see that clergy are not therapists,
they are not psychological technicians, they are not community mental health officers. They are *generalists*, and in the long
run, this is the more difficult role. Clinical learning through a
peer group experience under qualified leadership drawing on
the behavioral sciences enhances the abilities of the clergyman
as a generalist and helps him discover greater fascination and
challenge in his congregational ministry.

Consultation which is task-oriented and aimed at expanding workable knowledge and increasing the skills of effective
caregiving is one way of helping the professional minister reduce his personal preoccupation with institutional survival-
goals (responsibility for which normally should be shared
widely by members throughout the congregation) and focus
more of his energy and time on ministering with increasing
effectiveness to the valid human needs of his congregation and
community. Beginning with the identification and appraisal of
such needs the pattern of task-oriented consultation suggested
in this book is a valuable resource. The clinical training which
it provides allows a group of ministerial peers to multiply their
learning opportunities as they interact with their consultant
and with one another.

Dr. Henry B. Adams, Director of the Academy of Parish

Clergy, Inc., has argued strongly in favor of this kind of learning in his paper, "Consultation: An Alternative to Supervision." His concluding observation challenges us to extend the opportunity and multiply the consultative resources available to clergy:

> *Learning the practice from the practice* is vital in any profession that makes extensive use of art for its effectiveness. If clinical learning is to characterize continuously the professional life of clergymen, ways must be found to organize and facilitate that learning systematically. . . . If clinical learning is to be organized for ministers numbering in the thousands, in a massive attack upon their educational needs, better models will be needed.

The wider use and development of task-oriented consultation has many implications for churches and denominations, because it provides continuing clinical training for religious professionals. This in itself augments significantly the professional training already received in theological seminaries, but more importantly, it is a means of keeping institutionally oriented ministers deeply sensitive to human needs and to the most creative ways of meeting these needs. This type of clinical learning will enrich and stimulate the work of ministers, and the enrichment will bring deeper satisfaction and fulfillment in their work as ministers.

OTHER RESOURCES FOR PROFESSIONAL GROWTH

Task-oriented mental health is one of several resources available to ministers for professional development. While it is non-academic, field-oriented, and not exclusively intellectual in its orientation, it makes theoretical knowledge vital by applying it to an actual working situation. Doing more of this in other ways by the employment of other learning resources will simply hasten professional growth and will make continuous the process of revitalizing one's work life. I would now like to mention several other resources that seem to me to be closely related and worth the consideration of any clergyman who wants to grow in his professional work as well as in his personal life.

1. A basic resource for evaluating professional growth which is available to clergymen in an increasing number of places is that of *career evaluation*. This procedure usually combines the analysis of skills and interests with goal-setting in such a way as to capitalize on one's basic abilities. Involvement in career evaluation as an ongoing process helps a clergyman select types of work and avocations which are most likely to allow him to grow to his fullest potential. The process is reflective in that it evaluates past achievements. It is dynamic in that it motivates the individual to take charge of his own career and development in such a way as to accomplish those goals which will provide maximum satisfaction. It can also be viewed as a necessary prelude to just living. A good career-evaluation procedure will help the individual identify areas in which additional professional learning and personal growth should occur. It will offer both encouragement and stimulation for continuing development and will pave the way for the maximum use and enjoyment of such experiences as group clinical learning.

2. Several years ago certain leaders in the field of clergy training and theological education joined with a small group of dedicated parish clergymen to establish the Academy of Parish Clergy, Incorporated. This professional association was modeled after the Academy of General Medicine. Since its founding it has grown to some 700 members. Its emphasis is on continuing education and development, and it advocates the use of a collegial model of ministry as a way of stimulating growth and learning. Members identify the special areas in which they prefer to study, experiment, and learn. Where possible, the group is formed on a community or regional basis. In this program the clergyman's work is evaluated, criticized, and commented upon by his colleagues so that growth and new

learning can occur. Task-oriented mental health consultation is entirely congenial to the spirit of the Academy of Parish Clergy. Membership in the Academy has the great advantage of formally committing a minister to high standards of professional performance and helps him identify with others who share his commitment.

3. The creative use of the peer-group interaction and the effective use of many different types of consultation are becoming key factors today in establishing and developing professional standards for the clergyman's role. The successful employment of this valuable resource depends really upon a fundamental disposition or desire to learn how to make the correct use of consultation in general. The clergyman who is committed to achieving higher standards of performance must display the kind of openness that allows him to receive what the consultant has to offer. The good consultee has to be able to recognize his own dilemmas, his own areas of need, his own quandaries. He must then have the insight and ability to phrase the kind of sharp question and precise inquiry that will enable him to search for and come up with sharp answers and precise solutions. Good consultation almost always begins with the consultee. This is true whether the consultation requested is in architectural design, engineering and construction, or in program planning. The consultee must first of all be motivated to search; and he must know how to search. Just as in preparatory training for crisis intervention so in the use of consultative resources, there appears to be a learning gap: divinity schools and theological seminaries do not at the present time seem to be training students how to identify problems in which consultation can help nor are they being assisted in learning how to choose and make use of good consultants.

Experiencing good consultation through mental health consultation not only provides clinical learning but offers an additional benefit: the opportunity of learning the technique of being a skilled consultee; and mastery of this technique will open up, in turn, the possibility of using many different types of interdisciplinary consultation.

In summary, this book has focused on mental health consultation as a method of learning for church professionals. The method offers an educational opportunity which is quite distinct from continuing education programs sponsored by an academic institution or some other kind of learning center. In the past many such programs were usually remedial: that is, they were offered as a means of compensating for deficiencies in the normal theological education curriculum. Other programs of this kind specialized specifically in theological restatement or in up-dating theological background.

The distinct learning characteristic to which we are calling attention in mental health consultation is that the learning occurs specifically in relationship to tasks and responsibilities that are currently being fulfilled. The curriculum is provided by the people and situations which the pastor encounters in his daily work. The faculty consists of a colleague from another profession, a group of his peers who are prepared to risk exposure in order to learn, and the persons to whom these pastors are called to minister. The learning that occurs has two results: it sharpens professional skills and allows a clergyman to conduct himself in his professional role with greater confidence in and certainty about the value of his ministry. This experience in turn further clarifies his personal identity as a minister and caregiver in the community. Through this affirmation of himself and his work, the clergyman finds it easier to enter into more peer-group relationships. With less to hide, he has more to give.

Notes

PREFACE

1. Most of the case material is derived from records of individual and group consultation sessions conducted during the past four years. They have been altered to preserve confidentiality, and all names have been disguised.

CHAPTER I: BACKGROUND AND EVOLUTION

1. G. Gurin, J. Veroff, and S. Feld, *Americans View Their Mental Health* (New York: Basic Books, 1960).

CHAPTER 2: THE CLERGYMAN AS COMMUNITY MENTAL HEALTH WORKER

1. Quoted in W. B. C. Watkins, *Perilous Balance* (Princeton, N.J.: Princeton University Press, 1939), p. 66.
2. *Ibid.*, p. 110.
3. *Come Out, Come Out, Whoever You Are: The Community Return Service Unit of the H. Douglas Singer Zone Center,* thirty-minute film, a production of Chicago Educational Television Assn., Robert Kaiser, Rudyard Propst, *et al.*, presented on WTTW Chicago, December 8, 1969. Available from: NET Film Service, Audio Visual Center, Indiana University, Bloomington, Indiana 47401.
4. Ruth Caplan, *Psychiatry and the Community in Nineteenth Century America* (New York: Basic Books, 1969).

CHAPTER 3: MENTAL HEALTH CONSULTATION

1. Robert Burton, *The Anatomy of Melancholy,* Everyman Library (London: J. M. Dent and Sons, 1968), Vol. 1, p. 37.

CHAPTER 8: EVALUATION

1. *The Problems of the Priest: Have His Concerns Become the Church's Crisis?* (The Executive Council of the Episcopal Church, 815 Second Avenue, New York, N.Y. 10017, 1970).

CHAPTER 9: IMPLICATIONS FOR COMMUNITY MENTAL HEALTH

1. See Gerald Caplan, *The Theory and Practice of Mental Health Consultation* (New York: Basic Books, 1970), chap. 3.

2. Ruth Caplan, *Psychiatry and the Community in Nineteenth Century America* (New York: Basic Books, 1969).

CHAPTER 10: SUPPORT SYSTEMS

1. For a detailed account of crisis theory see Gerald Caplan, *An Approach to Community Mental Health* (New York: Grune & Stratton, 1961), and *Principles of Preventive Psychiatry* (New York: Basic Books, 1964).

2. For the sake of completeness, I must mention that many mental health problems are not currently being dealt with by existing care-giving organizations, and a community psychiatrist must also consider how best to organize outside the framework of such organizations populationwide support for people in need. This raises the whole question of fostering the development of informal self-help networks among people who share a common fate that increases their risk of mental disorder, such as widows, divorced people, drug users, families of suicides, old people living alone, and new immigrants. Our Harvard Laboratory of Community Psychiatry is currently most interested in this topic, but it would not be appropriate for me to discuss it in this chapter.

Index